What experts say about this book!

Did we need another book on how to write the college application essay? You'll answer a resounding yes after reading Writing Impressive College Essays by Aimee Weinstein. She presents the information you need to know in clear, easy-to-absorb chapters that cover all the bases of this formidable task. From Common Application essays to those unique supplemental prompts required by special institutions, this book will guide you to write your most effective application essay. If you know nothing of the process, you will become so much more confident — and if you have some awareness already, your engagement with this book will enhance your self-reliance. Basically, Aimee holds your hand as firmly or gently as you need while whispering, "Don't worry, you can do this."

– Cathy Colglazier, College Essay Tutor

Having worked in college admissions since the late '90s, I am always skeptical of new books about the admission process. Often they're filled with impractical suggestions that create more stress or gimmicks that rub admission officers the wrong way. This book, by contrast, is fantastic. It is filled with useful suggestions, valuable examples, and plenty of reminders that this is not a one-size-fits-all process. Dr. Weinstein's advice is both warm and wise. This book will surely help students not only write great essays but also minimize their stress. I will be ordering it for my clients and sharing it with my colleagues.

– Reena Kamins, Founder, College Career Life

This page is intentionally left blank

VIBRANT
PUBLISHERS
™

WRITING IMPRESSIVE COLLEGE ESSAYS

11 Sample Essays

Step-by-step
Explanations

Practical Exercises

Expert Tips

DR. AIMEE WEINSTEIN

Writing Impressive College Essays
First Edition

Paperback ISBN-10: 1-63651-176-7
Paperback ISBN-13: 978-1-63651-176-4

E-book ISBN-10: 1-63651-177-5
E-book ISBN-13: 978-1-63651-177-1

Library of Congress Control Number: 2023940520

This publication is designed to provide accurate and authoritative information in regard to the subject matter covered. The Author has made every effort in the preparation of this book to ensure the accuracy of the information. However, information in this book is sold without warranty either expressed or implied. The Author or the Publisher will not be liable for any damages caused or alleged to be caused either directly or indirectly by this book.

Vibrant Publishers books are available at special quantity discount for sales promotions, or for use in corporate training programs. For more information please write to bulkorders@vibrantpublishers.com

Please email feedback / corrections (technical, grammatical or spelling) to spellerrors@vibrantpublishers.com

For general inquires please write to reachus@vibrantpublishers.com

To access the complete catalogue of Vibrant Publishers, visit www.vibrantpublishers.com

Table of Contents

Dear Student/Parent/Tutor –

Thank you for purchasing **Writing Impressive College Essays**. We are committed to publishing books that are content-rich, concise and approachable enabling more students to read and make the fullest use of them. We hope this book provides the most enriching learning experience to write an impressive college essay.

If you have any questions or suggestions, feel free to email us at **reachus@vibrantpublishers.com**

Thanks again for your purchase.

– Vibrant Publishers Team

About the Author

Dr. Aimee Weinstein is a full-time professor at the Honors College at George Mason University, where she teaches undergraduate students research methods and writing. One of her focuses is working with Honors College students who will mentor first-generation students in local high schools to write their college essays. In that course, Dr. Weinstein helps students with community engagement and understanding the landscape of the college admissions process in order to prepare the students to do the important work of mentoring. Dr. Weinstein is also affiliated with INTO Mason, where she works with International Graduate students on their research writing, transition management, and other assorted aspects that characterize a move to a new culture and American university life. In addition, when it is safe to travel, she plans to lead a summer study abroad course on Japanese Arts and Well-being.

For the past year, Dr. Weinstein has been a faculty fellow with the Stearns Center for teaching and learning, focusing on issues of Anti-Racism and Inclusive Teaching, hoping to gather enough resources to not only enhance learning about these critical issues but also pilot some workshops to help faculty be intentional in their classroom practices.

Before moving to Northern Virginia in 2015, Dr. Weinstein lived for more than ten years in Tokyo, Japan where she taught first-year writing and research writing at Temple University, Japan. In addition to traveling throughout Asia, she advocated for women's education via the Japan Support Committee of the Asian University for Women in Bangladesh.

Aimee's publications include a study guide for the ACT essay, a fiction piece in an anthology about the concept of time, and a small book on humorous English translations of Japanese signs. Most recently she edited a book of her students' creative nonfiction pieces. Her other, varied publications are mostly out of Japan and include English-language travel and food journals.

This page is intentionally left blank

How to best use this book

Ideally you are reading this book the summer before your senior year of high school, which is the best time to think about your college essay. If not, it's okay! The important part is that you're getting started and the steps here can be completed at any time.

First, you should read the introduction so you know what it means to write a college essay and why it is important. If you can understand why it matters then you will definitely do a better job.

Next, read Chapter 1 which has all of the information about what goes into your main essay and how to begin. The last few pages of the chapter are questions to answer so you can brainstorm your best topic. Remember, everyone is different, so if you and a friend are both using this book, you'll come up with different answers so you can write completely different essays.

Really work on that brainstorming and answer the questions fully so that you're ready for Step #2: drafting that main essay. The chapter goes through your brainstorming questions and asks you to combine some questions so your topic can really shine through. By the time you've worked through Chapter 2, you'll be ready to revise your essay.

In Chapter 3 you will learn more about revising – specifically why beginnings and endings of essays are so important, and what you can do to make your beginning and ending really shine.

After you go through the first three chapters of this book, you should have a fairly well-polished main essay, and you'll then be ready to go to Chapter 4 and work on your supplemental essays. Not every school will require supplemental essays, but most do, so you'll find some important tips and tricks (and examples!) on how to do what the schools are asking you to do.

Chapter 5 covers the COVID-19 question, which is still available as of the 2023-2024 school year. Remember, you do not have to do it; it is optional. Only do it if you feel your response will add something significant to your application package.

Some schools do not fit into the traditional application mold, and if you are applying to one of those schools, then use Chapter 6 to work on the essays for those colleges and universities. While we do not cover every single case, we go through enough that you can apply your work to your non-traditional application.

In the final chapter of this book, Chapter 7, you will find 11 essays that my students wrote and used in their college application packages. The essays are given to you as they were submitted, so you might see something you do not like or that you feel is incorrect in them. Our goal in showing you these essays is to that essays can be imperfect; they just need to reflect your true story.

Remember, applying to college is a journey. It is stressful and often not fun. However, if you relax and understand that everyone who goes to college goes through this, then you can put it into perspective and see that not only can it be an enjoyable process, but can also be a good time for reflection and connection with your experiences.

We hope this book will serve as a guide for everyone involved. Best of luck!

Acknowledgement

The following students graciously permitted me to share their work throughout this book. I thank them for not only allowing me to go public with their essays, but also for their effort in writing, their willingness to work with me, and their grace as they went through this process. I wish them the best of luck in future endeavors!

- Daniella Abuzobaa
- Jenna Ashtar
- Alana Berlo
- Jamie Bol
- Jessica Daninhirsch
- Sarah Demeglio
- Ethan Dixon
- Julia Dixon
- Ian Gresenz
- Michael Himy
- Emmet Ledell
- Benjamin Pizof
- Sydney Weinstein
- Jackson White
- Nolan Wick

This page is intentionally left blank

Introduction

The best part about writing your college essay is that it signifies the very start of your process – the start of what will be the next phase of your education. Whether you plan to go to school near home or far away; choose a big school or a small one; play a sport or not, everyone begins with his or her main essay – *the college essay.*

If done well, writing the essay has the potential to be great fun. The essay can be interesting, exploratory, and even revelatory. Your job here is just one thing: to get your personality on the page so that it reflects your uniqueness and allows colleges to discern why they should pick you to attend their school. Your personality is yours alone and will distinguish you from other applicants. Figuring out how to do just that does not have to be stressful if you start by following the plans and tips and tricks given in this book. You really can enjoy the process!

I have been working with students on their college essays for over fifteen years. My students have gone to schools such as Dartmouth, Georgetown, and Rice University. I have helped students gain entry into the University of Wisconsin, Indiana University, and the University of California. Some students would like big schools and others would like small ones. But everyone has one thing in common: they all write an essay. My background as a professor of writing at George Mason University in Fairfax, Virginia, and my doctorate in the teaching of writing have prepared me to help students write the very best essays they can. Over time, I have learned that those essays express the very best of students' work so that the students emerge strong and proud. I've learned so much from students over the years and I'm delighted to share what I know.

Most students begin with the "main" essay but what really is it and why is it so important? Some of that has to do with the Common App (www.commonapp.org). If you are applying to colleges in the United States, you will likely use this website or the mobile app. Over 900 colleges and universities have signed on to accept applications via this website. And as part of this website, students must submit a 650-word essay.

In the past, every college had its own prompts, but since the advent of the Common App website, colleges and universities are more inclined to use and accept the website's prompts. The number one reason the main essay is so important is that most colleges and universities do not have the capacity to interview every applicant. **Admissions officers want a way to get to know the people who apply** to their schools and asking students to write about themselves has proven to be an excellent way to achieve that goal.

The main essay has always been an important part of every college application packet, but it has grown in significance in recent years since the COVID-19 pandemic. At the height of the pandemic, many colleges and universities in the U.S. decided not to consider standardized test scores such as ACTs or SATs. Students in the class of 2020 and 2021 had trouble even finding tests to take since most test centers were closed, so that made sense. Going forward, schools have decisions to make regarding the testing, and some schools choose to stay test-optional, while others plan to go back to requiring them. Please check the current requirements of the schools to which you're applying. There are rumors that the main essay has taken on more importance with the de-emphasis of testing. Regardless, it is important to focus on having a great essay.

The main essay, however, is not meant to be a listing of activities or achievements; nor is it a description of your home life or favorite something or other. It is imperative that you meet one goal: *get your personality on the page.*

A few years ago, I was listening to the Director of Admissions at Virginia Tech University address potential applicants and their families. She noted that it is the job of the Admissions department to "craft" a freshman class. Admissions officers have to determine who will be a good fit for the university and who has the greatest chance of succeeding at their school. They need a balance of musicians and scientists. They need some people who are likely to join various clubs and some who are interested in service organizations. In fact, they need some people who are interested in all of those things and also might have great leadership potential. Unfortunately, since most schools do not allow students to have an interview with Admissions, the college essay is how they sort of get to know each student.

Think of it this way: when looking through your package of application information, the Admissions officers have access to several things. They have your grades, the teacher and counselor recommendations, your test scores, and your activities list/resume. Your guidance counselor at your high school will include a reference together with a profile of your school – its demographics, including the number of students in the school and the graduating class, along with a description of the types of classes available at the school with your admissions packet to every college or university to which you apply. In that way, the Admissions people get a picture of you and your credentials within the scope of where you've come from. All of those things I've just mentioned are fixed. The freshman, sophomore, and junior grades are set, and the standardized test scores are generally complete by the time you apply. Even the recommendations are somewhat fixed. Obviously, you will ask teachers who know you well and see you in the best light to write the recommendations, but you do not have control over what they write.

The one place where you, the student, have control, is the essay. You get to decide what you want to share with the Admissions Committee. **You get to tell your story and why it matters.** You get to show them who you are, what you care about, and how you plan to be in the world both in college and beyond. This is where you can share your dreams if you have big ones, or your worldview, if that is important to you. YOU are the topic of the essay; it's not what you've done or even what you will do – it's YOU!

A reason writing a college essay becomes frightening for many students is that most high schools do not focus on the personal essay as a genre. Students are mostly taught to analyze literature, prove a historical point, write a lab report, and write an argument – all of those genres are extremely useful and crucial parts of writing, but the personal essay is not among them. Perhaps this is the first time you have been asked to write about yourself at all.

This guidebook is meant to help you with the process.

The book itself is divided into chapters that represent the parts of the college essay process you need to address. Chapter 1 is on the main essay. You will work on brainstorming exercises, idea suggestions, and potential topics, including addressing the prompts - or choosing your own prompt.

In Chapter 2, you will take some potential answers to your brainstorming questions, and put them together at the start of essays. Chapter 3 is all about short examples, and focusing on beginnings and endings of the main essay. I will show you introductions, paragraphs, and conclusions, as well as other parts of essays that work or don't work – along with commentary about why the sentences are placed the way they are. In Chapter 4, we will work on supplemental essays. These are school-dependent, but there are various ways to approach them in general, and you can explore those approaches, both in a specific sense as well as in a creative sense. In Chapter 5, you will see if and how you might approach the COVID-19 prompt that remains on the Common App website. Not all students will elect to write it, but the prompt does warrant consideration. In Chapter 6, we will look at supplemental essay questions that are outside of the range of normal questions. We will also look at a few schools that are not on the Common App at all and have their own application portals. This chapter will address both types of anomalies and how you might approach them.

Lastly, in Chapter 7, I'll introduce you to some essays that work. These are essays that are included here with the permission of their authors and are reproduced **without further editing. In other words, what you see here is exactly how the students submitted them and gained entry into the colleges and universities of their choice. The essays may have**

grammatical errors too. Remember, though, that these essays are complete and have been revised and edited. You might be tempted to compare your first draft to these finished products, but that is not helpful to you. We'll talk more in Chapter 6 about how to use the example essays to help you feel confident and not intimidated.

Let's get started! You can do this!

This page is intentionally left blank

Chapter 1

The Main Essay - Brainstorming

The main essay for your application, as we discussed in the introduction, is a reflection of you and your personality. The topic of the essay is YOU! The Common App website does give prompts to get you started if you want them, but there is no reason that you have to answer or address one of its prompts. You should feel free to write the essay that you want to write – the one that reflects YOU.

The main essay can be a maximum of **650 words** if you are submitting it via the Common App. If you are working with the Coalition App, as some schools require, then it's only 550 words maximum. While that seems a lot right now before you have started to write, the limit comes quickly when you really get going. Take a look at the introductory section of this book – it's nearly 1500 words, almost more than double the word limit and it doesn't seem long at all. You will not be able to go over the word count; the text box on the website will cut you off right at the limit. DO NOT write the essay directly on the website. Use a word processor or an application and then copy/paste the work into the text box. In that way, you don't risk submitting an incorrect essay and you have plenty of ways to edit, revise, and manipulate your text before submitting it. You can edit many many times on the application or word processor before entering the final text, and that is what you need to do; ensure that your work is as refined as it possibly can be before putting it up on the Common App website. You would not want to put something on the site with any errors in it.

The prompts given on the Common App website might serve as a spark for your work, and they are here:

1. Some students have a background, identity, interest, or talent that is so meaningful they believe their application would be incomplete without it. If this sounds like you, then please share your story.

2. The lessons we take from obstacles we encounter can be fundamental to later success. Recount a time when you faced a challenge, setback, or failure. How did it affect you, and what did you learn from the experience?

3. Reflect on a time when you questioned or challenged a belief or idea. What prompted your thinking? What was the outcome?

4. Reflect on something that someone has done for you that has made you happy or thankful in a surprising way. How has this gratitude affected or motivated you?

5. Discuss an accomplishment, event, or realization that sparked a period of personal growth and a new understanding of yourself or others.

6. Describe a topic, idea, or concept you find so engaging that it makes you lose track of time. Why does it captivate you? What or who do you turn to when you want to learn more?

7. Share an essay on any topic of your choice. It can be one you've already written, one that responds to a different prompt, or one of your own design.

(www.commonapp.org)

Please note that prompt #7 is a free-choice option – therefore, any essay you write is viable. You can choose whatever topic makes you feel good about yourself and your ideas. These prompts are meant to give you ideas, spark thoughts, and even open discussions – sometimes in classrooms – but you do not need to adhere to them strictly. Your job is to write the essay that best reflects your personality and sets you apart from other applicants.

Good College Essays - Examples and Topics

Why is it important here that the students mentioned here go to a science magnet school but do not write about science? Aha! It's important for Admissions counselors to see students as whole people, not just one facet of them.

It is important to remember that Admissions Officers read many essays and the ones that truly captivate the readers' interest from the beginning are with a strong opener. I worked with one student who loved running for the sake of it. She opened her essay with the sentence, "I don't know why anyone would wear headphones while running; you would miss everything." That one sentence helped the reader understand that she was not going to discuss running as a competitive sport as much as she would be more journey-focused. The opening sentence set out the writer's intention from the very beginning and intrigued the reader, which it was meant to do. The reader became invested immediately and wanted to read more.

Another example is one student who attended a STEM-focused school but wanted to discuss his acting in the school plays, so he opened with a brief description of himself on stage falling down on his knees, as required by the script, and how he worked so hard to make the action look natural while still preserving his joints. Another student at the same school opened with a scene in her kitchen with her sister as they cooked together. It's interesting to note that these students are steeped in scientific research as required for graduation from the school, but they chose to focus more on their home lives and what is important to them personally. That being said, I've worked with several students who became enthralled with their research over the course of their junior and senior years of high school, so they opened by describing that work, but then had to work very hard to make the rest of the essay about their thoughts, ideas, and feelings, not the research and its ups and downs. Some students wrote about the ups and downs of their research and how they handled the situation, and those worked well because they showed how they performed under pressure. But ultimately, the essays still had to focus on the students, not the work they performed.

What makes you, well, YOU? Think about that as you continue reading.

Another example is the student who used the main essay to talk about her research while working at the Smithsonian Institute's Natural History Museum in its butterfly exhibit. She opened her essay with a gorgeous description of walking into a garden and the butterflies swirling all around her but the ultimate point of her essay was that she has always been committed to environmental causes and cared deeply about the health of the Earth.

Another way to handle the main essay is thematically. I once worked with a student whose sport in high school was rifle shooting. Whenever young people handle a rifle, they must adjust their stances every time they grow a few inches, which happens often with teens. This particular student grew a foot, twelve full inches over the course of his junior year of high school. Add to that the mission trip he took to build houses in Asia the prior summer, and you have an entire essay built on the idea of growth: physical, mental, and spiritual.

One student came to me with her main essay already written, but she knew it wasn't quite right. It was a gorgeous description of being the prima ballerina in a production of the Nutcracker Ballet the year before. It had beautiful descriptions of the costumes, the music, the sets, and everything else, but there wasn't a word about her personally. The reader never knew what it took to get there, what it meant to her to have that role, and most importantly, why ballet wasn't something she intended to pursue in college. While we were able to keep a lot of her work, we had to add in quite a bit and pare down her descriptions in order to keep the word count to the right number.

> **TIP:**
> *The essay cannot be about something or someone you love – it has to be about YOU loving that thing or person.*

One student had spent most of his life, until his junior year of high school, living overseas and was balking at the idea of writing an essay at all. "Why can't I just say that I grew up in Asia?" he asked. "That's pretty cool." And while I agreed that it was super interesting, he still had to write an actual essay. He needed to find a way to discuss what made him who he is, a kid who felt part Asian though his heritage is 100% American. He ended up opening the essay with a description of traveling to Spain with his American high school orchestra and sitting in a restaurant where they ordered a plate of paella. When the food arrived, he picked up a huge prawn and put the whole thing in his mouth. Everyone shouted, "Eeewww, you just ate the whole thing!" and his response was, "Oh when I lived in Japan, we ate the heads." That allowed him to jump off into writing about his life in Asia being American, but moving to the U.S. at age 17, and all that it entailed. He did have to work hard to keep the essay about him and his feelings and not veer off into descriptions of Asia, but he got it in the end.

How to Begin

These are just a few examples of what you might think about writing in your main essay for college admission. Obviously, your journey is unique to you and unlike anyone else's. You have to think about who you are and what you want to convey. I'd recommend starting with the question, "What is it that I want Admissions Officers to know about me?" This is the one chance you have for the Admissions Committees to get to know who you are, what you value, and perhaps what you want to do in college and beyond. I hope these examples have gotten you thinking about what you want to say in your main college essay.

For most of your high school education, you have had analytical writing experiences. You have written about literature; you have proven points in an argument essay; you have written about historical events; and you have even written lab reports. Very few high schools focus on narrative writing and even fewer have students work on personal essays like this work requires. You have to start thinking about this essay as a new genre of writing; you are flexing a new and different writing muscle as you do this. There is no formula, and there is no right or wrong way to do it; there is only YOUR way of doing it and that is the right way for you personally.

When you're writing this essay, the temptation is to tell the Admissions people things about yourself. However, as you've seen in the examples above, and will see in the essays at the end of this book, everything works better if you show the readers what you mean, rather than just tell them. For example, if you are fearless, it's better to describe a time you acted fearlessly and reflect on it, rather than just state, "I am fearless." If you just tell someone something without evidence, he or she may or may not believe you. You're better off showing what you mean.

You must reflect and think before writing!

The ability to reflect is a very important tool for this type of task. When thinking about an event, you should ask yourself what the event means. What does it mean to others? Why was it important or why does it matter? What might you do differently in the future if you face the same type of thing? This is the essence of reflection, and a good college essay is a chock full of it. Show the readers something and then reflect on it. Show them something else and reflect on that. Tie the two things together and show how those two things form the base of your personality or something you really and truly value in your life. This is all about you – you cannot be wrong. Just keep writing – show and reflect.

Reflect → What does it mean → Why does it matter → What might I do differently?

A note of warning: you can look up college essays on the Internet easily. Indeed, there are several for your perusal at the end of this book. However, though they have the potential to give you many ideas for your own essay, it's also easy to get discouraged when you start comparing your first ideas or first draft to those polished essays that have been through many revisions already.

Brainstorming - Singular Questions About You

We are going to start here with some brainstorming first before you write. You will see a question, and then some space to write your answer. You will then be asked to combine questions and answer them so that perhaps some of the ideas give you further ideas to make into an essay. Not every question will pertain to you. The questions are meant to make you think about possible topics and consider ideas in a way that you have not done before.

It is important to really THINK through these brainstorming questions first and not think about an entire essay. Prewriting matters. In general, writing is 80% thinking and the rest is just words. Start jotting notes about the answers to these questions and see if something else comes into your mind. Keep writing and writing and writing. Do not worry about word count or other technical details until later in your process. First, think and doodle some words so ideas start flowing; then you can start to put ideas together into a structure you can work with.

Remember, the main college essay is NOT about what you do, what you like to do, or what you plan to do in the future. The main essay is about who you are, what you think about, what you believe, or other parts of your personality.

Start right here with this question:

If you could tell Admissions Officers of colleges and universities ONE thing about you, what might that one thing be?

Ex: My favorite place in the world is at my aunt's house in Texas. I feel most at home there - continue the story here!

_____

_____

_____

_____

_____

_____

_____

_____

_____

_____

_____

_____

_____

_____

_____

_____

_____

_____

Write down five activities that you do outside of school or before or after school.

Ex: church, choir, Best Buddies Club, racquetball — now pick one and write a few extra sentences about it!

_____

_____

_____

_____

_____

_____

_____

_____

_____

_____

_____

_____

_____

_____

_____

_____

_____

_____

_____

_____

_____

What did you do last summer? What do you plan to do this coming summer? Have you ever had a summer experience that changed you?

> *Ex: camp counselor last summer, grandpa's office this summer. Favorite summer that changed me was at camp realizing I love acting in plays. (now write a few sentences about the plays!)*

_____

_____

_____

_____

_____

_____

_____

_____

_____

_____

_____

_____

_____

_____

_____

_____

_____

Do you have brothers or sisters? Describe your family situation.

Ex: I do not have siblings, but I am close to my cousins and our family has dinner together every week (describe the dinner!)

_____

_____

_____

_____

_____

_____

_____

_____

_____

_____

_____

_____

_____

_____

_____

_____

_____

_____

_____

_____

_____

Have you ever taken a major family trip? Do you have a family trip that you take every year?

Ex: Every year, my family goes to the beach with all of my aunts, uncles, and cousins. (now write a few sentences about that trip!

_____

_____

_____

_____

_____

_____

_____

_____

_____

_____

_____

_____

_____

_____

_____

_____

_____

_____

What is your favorite food? Least favorite food? Why? Would you describe yourself as a "foodie?" Does food play into your family life in any significant way?

Ex: I love to cook with my mom even though I'm not the greatest eater (write a few sentences that describe your cooking and your mom).

_____

_____

_____

_____

_____

_____

_____

_____

_____

_____

_____

_____

_____

_____

_____

_____

_____

_____

_____

What, if any, volunteer work do you do? How does that play into your after-school activities?

> Ex: Even though I'm busy at school and I play a sport, I make time every month to volunteer at my church's food drive (now write a few sentences about what you do there and why).

_____

_____

_____

_____

_____

_____

_____

_____

_____

_____

_____

_____

_____

_____

_____

_____

_____

What is your favorite subject at school? Is it your best subject also? What makes you excited to work hard or learn more?

Ex: I love my history class and I do my best work there. I am fascinated with the Renaissance and read about it all the time (now describe what you love precisely and why).

_____

_____

_____

_____

_____

_____

_____

_____

_____

_____

_____

_____

_____

_____

_____

_____

_____

_____

_____

_____

Have you ever overcome a serious challenge? If so, what and how? (Be sure to focus on the overcoming part – not the challenge itself. In those cases, they want to know about your ability to overcome them!)

Ex: I had to move to a new country for my dad's work when I was in 10th grade. It was hard but…. (now write about how you got through it).

_____

_____

_____

_____

_____

_____

_____

_____

_____

_____

_____

_____

_____

_____

_____

_____

_____

_____

If a teacher was going to write only 3 things about you, what would he or she write?

> *Ex: My teachers know that I am a multifaceted person. Not only do I get good grades and participate in class, but I also have a really funny side and can keep our class periods lively. I love to make people laugh. (Keep writing on how you do it and why it matters to you)*

_____

_____

_____

_____

_____

_____

_____

_____

_____

_____

_____

_____

_____

_____

_____

_____

_____

_____

If you could spend a day doing just one thing, what would it be and why?

Ex: I love woodworking. I could spend all day with a lathe in my hands, designing and creating bowls. (Now go on to explain why it matters and how it makes your life better!

_____

_____

_____

_____

_____

_____

_____

_____

_____

_____

_____

_____

_____

_____

_____

_____

_____

_____

_____

Look around your room. Do you have one THING that is defining for you? What is it and why is it important to you?

Ex: my grandparents were away on a trip to Spain when I was born. They brought me back a snow globe and ever since, I have collected snow globes (keep writing about the globes and why they're important to you).

_____

_____

_____

_____

_____

_____

_____

_____

_____

_____

_____

_____

_____

_____

_____

_____

_____

_____

_____

Do you have a pet who you have loved your whole life? A new pet? How has that pet made a difference in your life?

Ex: I never thought I could love another pet after my dog passed away when I was in middle school, but then we got my cat, Mittens. (Keep writing about what pets mean to you).

_____

_____

_____

_____

_____

_____

_____

_____

_____

_____

_____

_____

_____

_____

_____

_____

_____

_____

_____

Why is it important for you to go to college – not just a particular university – but college in general?

For example, discuss how you are the first in your family to apply to college. Or that everyone in your family has gone to a particular place and now it's your turn. But maybe you just write about what you will do with a college education and why it is meaningful to you. That's a great way to approach the question.

_____

_____

_____

_____

_____

_____

_____

_____

_____

_____

_____

_____

_____

_____

_____

_____

_____

_____

Next: Combining Questions About You

Combine two or more questions – for example, how does your family life play into your love for food?

Ex: "My family loves to travel and to us, that means trying different types of food. Whenever we go on a trip, we take turns figuring out where to eat." From here you might go on to describe your family's trips and the food and your role in all of that.

_____

_____

_____

_____

_____

_____

_____

_____

_____

_____

_____

_____

_____

_____

_____

_____

Now combine two more questions: for example, how do any of your summer experiences play a role in your love for learning or love for a specific topic?

Ex: "For the past two summers I have gone to a camp to learn cooking skills." Now you can go into why you love cooking and what it means to you – as well as why you spend your summer free time doing it!

_____

_____

_____

_____

_____

_____

_____

_____

_____

_____

_____

_____

_____

_____

_____

_____

_____

_____

_____

_____

Now again combine two more questions: for example, does that defining thing that you wrote about in the prior question, have to do with something you could do or enjoy for 24 hours straight? What makes it special?

> *Ex: "My snow globes are all over my room and they make me remember all of my trips. After college, I would like to be a travel agent and open my own business. I could spend all day helping people love to travel as much as I do." Keep going here!*

_____

_____

_____

_____

_____

_____

_____

_____

_____

_____

_____

_____

_____

_____

_____

_____

_____

Next Steps

If you can answer these questions - or most of them - then you are well on your way to your main essay topic. The next chapters will show you what to do with your ideas and how to craft them into fully formed-main essays.

This page is intentionally left blank

Chapter 2

The Main Essay - Drafting

Now that you've done all of that great brainstorming, let's take some potential answers to your brainstorming questions, and put them together at the start of essays. Remember, essays take many drafts, so the first thing you write will not be the final essay. Sometimes these things take five or six tries until they flow well and sound final.

Starting any essay is never simple. You can stare at a blank page on your computer for a long time and not write a single word. I want to encourage you to write a few words. Anything will do. Get started. Write a joke. Write a funny story you just heard – write anything that will get you started. It is always infinitely easier to fix work that is at least partially done than to just figure out starting later. Try your best not to procrastinate and just get started. Write down a few answers to the brainstorming questions. Think how you can combine the questions from the first chapter and how you might make yourself stand out from the crowd.

This chapter will help you see the first drafts of essays, how the students answered the questions, and then started writing the essay.

Example #1 – Combining Questions

1. What do I want the Admissions Committees to know about me and what is my family situation?
    I have a special needs sister and because of her, I want to be a teacher of students with special needs.

2. What did I do last summer?
    Last summer I volunteered at a camp where my older sister is a camper.

This student has an interesting situation and the advice she was given was to start writing paragraphs. She wanted to write one about her sister, one about her camp volunteering experience, and one about being a teacher. The student's concern was that the paragraphs would not connect well but her first job was to write the paragraphs and then she could write in what we call "connective tissue" to make sure that the paragraphs flow together. What you see here is just a collection of sentences she put together to start out with each paragraph.

Alert: the essay below is a draft only, not a final version. Watch for how it is about the sister and not enough about the writer. She has moments of **showing** herself, but not too many. How might you change that?

First Draft (Student Essay)

My sister has always been different from other people's big sisters. She can be really funny and laughs really loudly and I can tell her any joke and she will immediately laugh. She tells jokes too. She likes to put a colander on her head and pretend that it's armor and she's a warrior. She sometimes wants to wear makeup and she sometimes wants to wear sweats. But my sister Anna is different. She was deprived of oxygen at birth and it has affected every part of her development. Still, she is my sister and we are best friends.

Last summer I got to volunteer at the summer camp where Anna has gone since she was 5 years old. I wasn't a counselor exactly but I helped in a bunch of ways. My favorite thing to do at the camp was work at the tennis courts. Anna has always liked to hold a tennis racket but can't really see well enough or have the depth perception to figure out when the ball is coming and get ready to swing. I have had so many tennis lessons in my life and I am the captain of my high school tennis team that I sometimes like to just stand near her and toss the ball right to her racket to hit. It makes her so happy. And so that's where I stayed most of the time during my four weeks of volunteering. The kids at Camp Connelly range in age from 5-20 and have all sorts of challenges, but mostly they are just kids who want to come together to have a good time and maybe learn some new skills. I'm just any regular kid but these kids are special. They always have a smile for me. They always want to braid my hair or ask me how I feel. It only took me a few weeks to figure out that even though I thought I was helping them, they were really helping me. They missed a ball and they didn't care.

They felt hot but they didn't complain. One boy I met was about twelve and he wanted me to stand close and just toss the ball so he could hit it with the racket. He would have spent three hours at the tennis court if they let him.

These campers taught me about laughing in the face of adversity. I learned about helping others. I discovered how fun it is to just help someone succeed however they can. And most importantly I learned how success doesn't look the same for every single person.

All of those lessons made me want to be a teacher of special needs students. When I think about the love and joy I felt every day during my summer, I feel like a career with these types of people would be the best thing I can do for not only me, but for kids like my sister Anna. And that's what I hope to study in college.

When you show something with details - don't just say "they helped me" but give concrete examples that are tangible to the reader - it makes you sound creative and thoughtful

The essay above is such a great start! But, I have many questions and suggestions for the student. She's mixing ideas in paragraph two – it should be more about the camp than about her sister. In the first paragraph, she mentions that she and her sister are best friends. I would like to see that – she should SHOW it – be more sensory in her work. She can write a scene that shows her and her sister talking or interacting in some way so the reader can really feel the relationship between the two of them, otherwise just telling it to the readers does not ring true. I would recommend a few sentences that show them doing something together besides tennis, something that is highly personal to them. For example, "Even now as teenagers, we like to snuggle up together in Dad's big recliner to watch TV together. He never complains when we squish our bodies together in his chair because he loves how close we are. He even sits on the sofa to watch whatever silly teen show we're into at the moment." If you read that sentence a few times, you can infer some details about the family, such as their closeness and willingness to be together, which reads much more truthfully than simply "My sister and I are best friends." The showing of the chair and the dad involved gives off an aura of connectedness that the reader can feel.

The advice I like to give at this point is: show, don't tell. What are you hearing? Touching? Smelling? Be sensory!

Similarly, readers need a sense of the camp too. Perhaps the writer can elaborate on the tennis court and what it looks like or how long she stayed there per day or even how many kids she helped in a day. Any details would give the piece some texture so that the ideas pop off the page and are believable. In addition, the student sort of "throws in" that she wants to teach special needs students. It needs more of a build-up or some more context and details. These are all easily fixable situations and the student will have a fun time revising her work into a strong essay.

Practice here:

Write a paragraph about a person in your life with whom you share a special relationship. A parent, a teacher, an aunt, anyone. How might you SHOW a relationship with a person but make the work about YOU and not just that person? What objects might represent that relationship? What sensory details could you include?

_____

_____

_____

_____

_____

_____

_____

_____

_____

_____

_____

_____

_____

_____

_____

_____

Example #2 – Combining Questions

1. What is your family situation?
   It seems like everyone in my family is a civil engineer and builds buildings.

2. What is the one thing you want to learn/do all day?
   I want to work on computers all the time, as much as possible. And if I can't design software, I want to build actual computers. But I do not want to build buildings.

3. What do I want the Admissions Committees to know?
   I am a family-oriented person, but I'm also really independent.

One way to begin: one paragraph at a time! You can always write "connective tissue" - i.e. transitions - later!

This student has a great story to tell so she has to organize it in a way that makes sense to her purpose. The readers want to know that she has a passion, but it doesn't match the passions of her parents or other family members. You might be wondering why that matters, but it really does – and it makes for an interesting essay that will help the Admissions Committee see not only who she is but what she values. The trick will be getting all of it into just 650 words and a few paragraphs.

In this case, I recommend that she writes one paragraph on family values, one on her own passion, and then a third on the mashup (or not!) between the two. This is a draft, not the final essay so you can see how the student began the work. The paragraphs do not necessarily flow together yet, but they will after some revising.

As you read this draft, notice the details. The student uses a lot of descriptions. Is it necessary? How much is too much?

First Draft (Student Essay)

Sometimes just for fun, my parents like to take my younger brother and me to see buildings that they think are cool. Both of my parents are civil engineers and met in college while doing their degrees, so building stuff is their passion. It used to be kind of fun to hop in the car on a Saturday to see what was happening around our town. We'd go past construction sites where the cranes and bulldozers sat and my parents would guess what grade of concrete they were using depending on how high the building would end up being. My brother always watched the trucks; he was fascinated with trucks. He would even point them out on the road and wonder where they were headed. We don't live in a huge town, so there wasn't always a construction site to go to, but sometimes my parents would even take us into the nearest city, 20 or so miles away, just to look at construction sites. Dad has worked at the same company forever designing heating and cooling systems for buildings while Mom has jumped around a little between jobs because her passion is making buildings energy efficient, which is a newer specialty. It seems clear that my younger brother is going to do something in the field also, since his interest in trucks still hasn't gone away and he's already 14.

For me, the Saturday trips around town stopped being fun by the time I was 12 and got my first computer that was just mine to use and figure out, not the family computer. I think my parents got it for me for Christmas that year because I kept trying to figure out how stuff worked on the machine in the kitchen all the time and they didn't want their stuff messed up anymore. I played computer games, sure, but I always wanted to know how the computer games worked. How did *the program know that I wanted to turn right in the first-person game? How did the keystrokes I used get the character to move and do stuff? How did the treasure chests in the game appear? With the computer came a suggestion to download Scratch, a pretty easy programming language, and that was it. I was hooked. Scratch led to Java which led to Python and I've been programming ever since. I've done all sorts of stuff for school, for home, for fun and just to play around with friends. It has never been all about gaming but about being productive and making stuff so other people can be too. It's always hard for me to get off the computer – or stop tweaking my latest program – and get moving on my actual homework.*

My parents are baffled. They spend a lot of time trying to force me out of the house and away from the computer. They think buildings and work in real life is much more exciting and I should be spending time on that. They still want me to get out into the world and touch things and build stuff because that's what they like. What they still don't understand is that I can build stuff that is just as important and interesting while sitting in my room or in the living room working on the computer. Computer models are the basis of what they use to do the actual building plans. I can program the heck out of whatever I want to ask the computer to do for me. The best part of computer programming is that it can be used for a million different things. I am not sure what specific part of programming I want to go into while I'm in college, but I'm sure I'll figure it out.

In the meantime, I'm sure my parents will get over it and they have another kid to try to indoctrinate into the civil engineering world. Although at the rate he's going, I wonder if he will be a truck mechanic. Keep trying parents.

Sometimes the hardest part of writing is knowing what to leave out. My advice is to start with adverbs - anything that ends with "ly" can usually be eliminated!

This student also has a great start! Unlike the prior student, she is already over the word count of 650 words and will have to make adjustments. Please note that I did not say simply cut words. Cutting words out is the very last thing students should do with their essays. It is important to start with just getting ideas down on the page and revise from there.

I would like to start here with a few grammar suggestions. First of all, the student often uses a past participle verb tense that involves "would" a lot. Instead of saying "would take us" the student should say "took." It's a simple fix that automatically eliminates words. A search in the document for the word "would" will allow the student to carefully make the fix in each instance. In addition, the student should go through her essay and make sure the language says exactly what she means. Does she want to "program the heck" out of something? I think she can use better language. Something along the lines of "I can finesse a computer program to achieve whatever result I desire" might be more on par with what an Admissions Committee would expect language-wise.

Pro Tip:
Revise your language to make it more on a par with what an Admissions Committee would expect - here are some examples.

- *do = achieve*
- *answer = result*
- *use past tense rather than "would" formats*
- *get = receive*
- *OR get = understand*
- *problem might = challenge*
- *avoid "stuff" if possible - "things" might be better*
- *next might = ensuing*
- *Find the forms of the verb "to be" - is-words, linking verbs, and change them to active verbs.*
- *Do not use any sort of slang or acronyms that you might use with friends*
- *On the other hand, if you use big words that are not in your normal vocabulary, you will not sound like yourself. Use good judgment there.*

The student does a great job being sensory in parts of the essay with the discussion of the construction sites and being in her parents' car with them as they speak excitedly. I can get a picture in my head of what that's like. I can also see a young student fiddling around on a computer and the ensuing parental frustration that would lead them to buy a single-user machine for a budding programmer. Those are good feelings to show, rather than just telling the reader, and the student does a good job with it here.

In this case, the first paragraph is very long. At the end of the day, 650 words is not that much and it's important to have a balance of paragraphs so that they're interesting and not overwhelming. The student might want to break the paragraph into two smaller ones. She might think about what information is most important to convey about her parents and her childhood. Remember, the point here is to get the student's personality onto the page and help the student stand out, so it's important to focus on what the student does, likes, or feels. The information about her parents and brother is secondary.

☞ **Reminder:**
The primary goal is YOUR personality on the page!

I would love to know more about what attracts the student to programming. What is it that she loves so much? How did her first attempts go? How has she progressed and what is she doing outside of playing around to fuel her passion? Did she go to a class or a camp? I'm not sure if all of that information will fit into this format, but it is important to know what questions to ask yourself as a follow-up to the initial brainstorming questions. The first question you should always ask yourself is how can you make this essay more about what you think and believe.

As noted previously, the student has a great story to tell and this is a great start. She should be encouraged to keep going forward with it and adding pertinent details while adjusting grammar and taking away details that are less relevant.

Example #3 - Single Question

1. If you could do one thing all day, what would it be and why?
   READING!

Sometimes there is a question that is so perfect for a student that he or she has to answer it. This one student is a reader – he spends all of his free time reading. He will be able to put in a little bit about his family situation because his parents influenced him to read a lot, but in general, his essay will be about reading. That being said, the student cannot simply list books or show what he likes to read or how he grew up reading so much. He has to find an angle, a way to get not only WHAT he does but WHO he is onto the page via the idea of books. That is a bit tougher, but the student can begin by writing chronologically about how reading influenced him over the years. He can write a paragraph about books he enjoys and why. He can write another paragraph about what books mean to him and why. He has to remember that the essay can begin with disparate paragraphs and he can worry about a connective tissue later – this is a first draft.

☞ *Reminder:*
Reflection is not only WHAT you did, but why it matters and why it is or was important!

First Draft (Student Essay)

My parents read to me a lot when I was little. I was not a rambunctious little boy in the traditional sense, and sitting quietly to read or flip through pages of picture books was always a particular pleasure, but when my mom or dad invited me into their laps to read to me, I took the opportunity every time. In fact, I think my parents read to me long after I could read for myself. When I was able to get through short chapter books in second grade, my dad still sat on my bed and read Harry Potter books to me chapter by chapter over long stretches of time.

In sixth grade my mom found a parent-child book group at the library for us to join. Some months my mom, an English teacher, would go, and some months my dad, a history professor, would go with me and my younger sister, who also loved it. That's where I learned about books about dragons, aliens, and alternate universes. While my sister drifted off into an all-girls, mother-daughter version, I stayed with the more diverse group for a few years.

It took a little while, but by ninth grade I found my niche. Though I don't really identify as a writer, I read so much that I figured out I'm a good editor and joined the literary magazine and the newspaper as editorial staff. I'm pretty good at noticing how words fit together and how sentences come together to create a story.

Some guys have trouble because they're not into sports or they don't fit a typical "guy" mold. I never had that problem, most likely because my parents are really supportive of whatever it is that I want to do. I know who I am and what I can do, as well as what I really like. I still read a lot. I read a ton of mysteries and fantasy novels, but over the years my palate has extended into nonfiction too. I love books by journalists about historical figures they've interacted with. I like politicians' autobiographies. I even like just straight-up history books. Sometimes I read to learn and sometimes I read to be entertained.

What am I going to do with all this reading? I still don't know exactly. Editing and publishing are a real possibility. Straight-up journalism is still on the table. But wherever I go next, it will definitely involve books in some form.

Look back on the essay above one more time. Does it need to be in order from beginning to end? Maybe not. Think about a way you might mix it up in time. What do you think is the most important event that might come first?

This is a really short first draft, but there are a lot of ways to fix it. First of all, even though it was suggested above and is often a great place to start, chronology as a structure does not work in all cases. For example, first this happened, then that happened. It's not always interesting to the reader and sometimes you need to shake it up and work backward, or even start in the middle of a story. There is more information on beginnings and endings in the following chapter but just keep in mind that jumping around in time is often okay for a personal essay.

Additionally, this essay might have too many parts to it. It could be an essay on what he likes to read or how his parents shaped his reading habits. But do we need to know about his sister and her reading history? Probably not – he can leave that part out. In addition, he sort of "throws in" the part about being okay with being a reader and not a "typical" guy. It's unclear what he means by that and he does not go into detail at all. What does typical even mean and how did the writer know he wasn't typical? How did he become okay with not being typical? What led him to try the literary magazine or newspaper in the first place and how did he discover it was his niche? He could go into a lot more detail on how he has progressed in his work on both the magazine and the newspaper since he was a freshman. Has he assumed any sort of leadership position there? While Admissions Committees can find details about what he did extracurricularly in high school from his activities resume, details and explanations are sometimes useful in the essay.

Details details details - they are important. Certain words like "typical" need to be explained further. Choosing which details matter and which do not is quite a trick, but worth your time to think about what the Admissions Committee really needs to know about you!

The specific advice I would give to this student as he moves forward is to really think about what he wants the Admissions Committee to know about him and what does he really want to highlight here? While answering just the one brainstorming question and not adding others into the mix, he has lost the opportunity to write a fuller and more engaging essay. Remember, it's not only about the WHAT you do but the WHO you are that matters to an Admissions Committee. In addition, they often focus on what makes you as a candidate stand out from other candidates, so if this student focuses solely on reading and books, he misses another opportunity to stand out from any other reader who writes his or her essay about books.

This first draft is a great start and I do not want to minimize the importance of the student's experiences, as well as his commitment to the broad topic he discusses. Details are needed and ways to connect paragraphs to each other are crucial. A more focused decision on the scope of the topic will be a first start. Remember, getting something down on the page is a great way to get the conversation started. It is always easier to edit work that has begun than to start afresh.

Drafting an essay is not particularly easy. It takes time, effort, and planning. I like to tell my students that writing is 80% thinking and the rest is just words. However, words need to be in the right order and understandable, which is the intimidating part. Just remember that no one ever gets the work right on the first try. Everyone needs drafts and an editor; even great writers like Stephen King or J.K. Rowling.

Revision is an important part of any writing process. Think of it this way: REVISION = Re/Vision. Re is the Latin prefix that means "again" and "vision" and its Latin root VIS, means "to see". Therefore, revision literally means to "see again."

RE/VISION - to see again

We're not talking about just fixing some grammar points or adjusting punctuation so it works. Your job after the initial drafting is to look at what you have written and then see it again. You should put down your essay and give it a little time before you look at it again so that when you go back to it, you have fresh eyes. If you give this process enough time, you will be successful.

Think here:

If you were writing an essay about your favorite activity or event, what details are the most important to include? Why? How do you know?

_____

_____

_____

_____

_____

_____

_____

_____

_____

_____

_____

_____

_____

_____

_____

Chapter 3

Breaking Down the Main Essay - Beginnings and Endings

In this chapter, we will look at a few paragraphs of various main essays, and I can show you what went right, what needed improvement, and where the main essay went from that point. Once you have worked on the brainstorming questions from the prior chapter and decided on your main essay topic, it is important to stay focused on the main essay and make sure that it follows your theme or gets your real personality on the page. This section mostly focuses on the beginnings and endings of essays since those are the most important parts of an essay – you want to start strong and end well.

Openings of essays draw the reader's attention to the topic, but more importantly, draw the reader into the topic. The opener makes the reader want to read the rest of the essay. It should have an interesting language, a description, or an allusion to what will happen in other paragraphs. Please do not think of it as something academic that needs a thesis statement. You are not proving a point here; rather you are introducing yourself to an Admissions Officer or Committee, so a formal sentence that indicates the topic of the paper is not needed. However, an idea of what the essay will cover is always a good idea. In that way, the reader will really want to keep reading.

Example 1: Draft of the Opening Paragraph of a Main Essay That Draws in the Reader

I am a local celebrity. Before you get too excited, I am a celebrity to a gang of 8 year old girls at my local pool, Hamlet Swim Club. Imagine this: it's 8 am, you're stepping out of your car when you hear the shrill chants of your name coming from 100 feet away, but when you turn around seven, 8 year old girls, buns on top of their head, body slam into you as their attempt to hug. Every coach has a drive, a desire to curate the best possible athlete, push them to their boundaries, and is there, every practice, because they want to give back to a sport that they love. However, not every coach gets the pleasure of having a mini army of swimmers who have progressively morphed into an 8 year old version of themselves.

Essay specialist comment:

Though super fun and visual, the intro is a bit long and though you are more than fifty words into the essay, you still have no idea what it is about and what it is really saying about the student. The student went on to cut some words from this introduction and bring in her point. That being said, her ending has her point clearly laid out even from this first draft.

Pro Tip:

You want your introduction to explain your point, but it cannot be too long because your essay is relatively short. How might you introduce your essay topic concisely?

Example 2: Draft of Ending Paragraph of a Main Essay That Clearly Lays Out the Point of the Essay

I find my happiness, no matter what mood I am in, from the smiles of the kids. Being the spotlight in someone's life has taught me to project more positively because those around me are going to mimic my every motion. One thing I struggle with is I beat myself up when I don't fulfill an expectation or goal, but now that I have all these younger kids, who don't know how to react in a situation when they are frustrated, watching me, and I have to show them that it's ok and to take fallen experiences as a chance to work harder to reach their goal

Essay specialist comment:

I really like this sentiment. You need to work on the wording a little so that it comes out more clearly – I had to read it three times. Maybe more like, "I see kids beat themselves up when they are frustrated with their performance, and while I did the same thing at their age and sometimes still have to remind myself not to do it, I know being a role model means…

I am telling these kids to take a hit as a learning opportunity and not be upset with themselves, so why should I not be doing this to myself in my own life? Being forced to project this positive outlook has caused me to believe it more and more every day, and I have taken great strives to the way I react to failure. I now ask myself will this matter in 5 years, 5 weeks, 5 days or even 5 hours?

Essay specialist comment:
I like this and I like what it brings to the ending.
It's almost like you are working on a zen sense of balance.

Making choices to listen to my own advice has shaped me into who I am today and who I want to continue to be.

Pro Tip:
Even though you want to use strong and appealing language, you want to avoid complexity and needless confusion in your sentences. Be direct and clear.

Can you see what she is striving to tell you? The student is trying to say that she wants to be a role model to kids – and then takes her own advice that she's so good at sharing with little kids. The essay turned out to be very successful because she could poke a little fun at herself while still explaining some serious ideas! The ending of an essay needs to leave the reader with something important. It can be a bit amusing, but it has to be thoughtful and interesting.

Essay endings are really important! Leave your readers with a great feeling or sense of wonder or something warm and special.

Another student here has a pretty serious message to convey and in order to show you the seriousness of it, given here are the first three paragraphs of her first draft of the main essay.

Example 3: Draft of First Three Paragraphs of a Main Essay

As my legs shakingly pushed me up during mid squat, I finally stood up straight carrying the 200 pound weight on my back, I looked in the mirror in front of me, and a huge smile plastered across my face as tears came down the sides of my cheeks because I no longer saw the girl I used to see in the mirror

Essay specialist comment:
What if you put something in here like "I wished I could go back and talk to my nine-year-old self". Then that would be the jumping off point to tell the story more concisely.

That nine-year-old girl As a shy, quiet and insecure person [sic], I lacked passion and the will to change. I felt weak in the mind and body. I struggled with my body image and felt self conscious about the way I looked relative to societal expectations. This was during those awkward middle school years where my body was changing and my weight was fluctuating which further exacerbated my feelings of insecurity.

At the age of 9 I had been diagnosed with ADHD, therefore I started taking adderall to help me academically during school, given I had struggled largely when having a learning disability. The medicine had become my worst enemy: It had taken a toll on me physically and mentally as I grew up. It started out as a pit feeling at the bottom of my stomach that was telling me I'm not hungry, so I didn't eat.. for hours that could turn into a full day. That full day of not eating was accompanied by the insomnia I had developed that had led me to having no energy or motivation for the next day. These unhealthy symptoms caused by the medicine had taken over my life starting at the age of 9 years old.

Some students feel that it is too big of a risk to discuss their big problems or their educational mishaps, and perhaps in some cases, it is.

However, the main essay is a place where some academic things can be explained or put into context. The very big key, which this student took to heart, is showing right at the start how the big problem, particularly an educational challenge, is overcome, or in the process of being put behind her.

Pro Tip:

If you have a particular academic challenge, address it. Own it. Explain it. But be brief about the problem itself; focus the essay on how you overcame the issue or are working on overcoming it. That shows Admissions committees that you are a strong and committed person.

The opening of the essay was particularly important because right away, the student needed to show how she was not only discussing her biggest challenge but intended to overcome it. Overcoming a challenge is a big theme in the world of college essays, and if done well, it can explain a lot and show a big plus to the Admissions Committee – resilience is a wonderful trait. Here's how the first draft of that essay read in final form.

Example 4: Final Form of Main Essay

I renewed my self assurance and began with weight lifting to strengthen myself .My high school's leaderboard gave me the motivation, determination and drove my personal goal to get on the board. In addition, I joined a club that I manage today, called Fit 4 Life. This club has many young people who also share similar challenges and want to do something to self improve. The club has afforded me the opportunity to share my experiences and support others who are just starting on this lifestyle journey. When I look back, I realize how far I've come in a short time. I recognize now the influence adderall had on me personally and the self conscious body image it created. I felt ashamed when I let my medication define me as a person and how it dictated my daily choices since I was a kid. Today, as my 17 year old self, I would tell my 9 year old self that I need to fight for myself and learn how to love myself. It took me eight years to get to where I am today. I have never felt stronger in the mind and body than I feel today, I have overcome my biggest challenge

Essay specialist comment:

Good ending. Let's work on some more of the wording and perhaps make the ending a little less final - you are not yet the person you will become!

She ends with a beautiful sentiment – it is strong and resilient. But I did want her to keep in mind that she is young and still becoming – nothing is yet final in her life. Keep that in mind, too!

**NOTICE THE SECTION ABOVE - A REVISION OF THE ESSAY ENDING. IT IS VERY FOCUSED ON THE OVERCOMING - NOT ON THE ACTUAL PROBLEM.

Write a paragraph here about a challenge, but only write one of the sentences about the challenge itself. The rest of the paragraph should be about how you overcame it.

_____

_____

_____

_____

_____

_____

_____

_____

_____

_____

_____

_____

Example 5: Draft of Main Essay Introduction

Although my old piano teacher owned two pianos, she preferred to bark instructions from her seat instead of using her other piano to teach at my side. Yet my new teacher does instruct me from his second piano. He'll explain what he's looking for in a passage, I'll play it, and then he'll play it back. We'll play back and forth until I've infused his suggestions on my own, and we'll move to the next section. By playing next to me, my new teacher leaves me empowered with a new perspective rather than feeling even more bemused than before. He doesn't know it, but my new teacher employs the EDGE method, an acronym that has guided me throughout my own teaching opportunities.

Essay specialist comment:

The introduction above is another one of my favorites because it is strong, interesting, and captivating, as well as gets right to the point.

This student is an Eagle Scout, a swimmer, and an accomplished pianist. However, he also really enjoys teaching all of these skills to younger kids. He wanted to write about all of that but didn't want to be cliché in his work. Therefore, he combined it all by describing a teaching method called EDGE (Explain, Demonstrate, Guide, Enable) to bring together all of the facets of his life. When he discusses each part, he shows how he uses the EDGE method to not only engage in the activity but also to teach it to others.

To notice:

The last sentence of the introduction functions as a thesis statement almost - you can tell that the essay will go on to explain the EDGE method. Be on the lookout for how to do just that - guide the reader and help the reader see the roadmap to your essay.

Here's the ending of his essay where he ties it all together.

Example 6: Draft of Main Essay Ending

The hardest part for me whether I'm teaching or learning is being patient. When using the EDGE method to teach, it takes a while for the skill to set in, which tests both the mentor and the mentee. As for learning, the strenuous job of creating a habit from a skill quickly takes over the initial excitement of learning that new skill. Making an ability routine takes time, but it benefits in learning more advanced skills and retaining them for a lifetime. Nevertheless, reminding myself to trust the system keeps me focused on the goal.

Now that I've completed the journey to Eagle Scout, I'm prepared to take on a leadership role, give first aid, or even make a tripod using lashings. Of all the skills I've learned, the EDGE method will serve me well. I haven't used those lashings anywhere in the real world yet, but they served as a great way to practice an approach to teaching that has guided me in my activities today and will continue to in the years to come.

Both the beginning and the ending of this main essay are remarkable and should be memorable to the readers. How might you make your opener and closer memorable?

Skillfully, this student makes it clear that he is on the cusp of his learning experience. Somehow the voice he uses in his essay makes him sound accomplished, yet humble. He explains his meaning, what he has learned, and sums up the work well. He refers back to the point he made at the beginning of the essay. And lastly, he has achieved the goal of the essay - putting his personality onto the page, in a very successful way.

Example 7: Draft Main Essay Introduction

This next student was very hesitant to use a family dinner discussion as an opener, but it ended up working really well because it was a good introduction to not only the theme of the essay but also served as an insight into the student's unique family life.

"Pass the Salad Olivier, please." My dad passes me a bowl of grandma's potato salad and starts talking about how lithium demand is increasing, and I remark on how a lithium mine stock released its IPO and how it will affect Tesla's batteries.

"Ben, stop staring at your food," my mom says, but I was repulsed by the fish head on my plate; its eyes stared me down.

As I attempt to eat the "food", my dad and I discuss the next big stock to buy and global politics. My dad rarely attends family dinners and eats the Russian dishes that comprise my family repertoire. I like to discuss business around the world with him, even if I don't like the food.

My family is filled with entrepreneurs reaching back to my ancestors in Russia. Nights like this are typical in our household, fueling my curiosity about the field.

To cement my interest in business, I attended a leadership program called Pennsylvania Finance Enterprise Week (PFEW), and I learned that in addition to spreadsheets and financials, leadership is a big part of entrepreneurship.

The point here is that the student was able to do many things with this essay. He opened with a family dinner scene because his family is so important to him, AND it's the place where he first learned to discuss business and finance – the things he is now passionate about and wants to study in college. The opener pulls the reader into the story – what this essay is about. Then, just as the reader is getting a little overwhelmed with the Russian dishes and wondering where the essay is really going – WHAM – the point is there: the student wants to go to business school. It is a very skillful opener.

Pro Tip:
This student uses present tense verbs when he talks about his family and past tense verbs when he talks about prior accomplishments. Use your words to help your essay flow!

The ending worked just as well – combining the week that the student spent at an exclusive business school learning experience and sharing that experience with his interested family members. He stays with his point that he is uniquely qualified to attend business school, but also re-introduces his family to tie the ending back to the beginning:

Example 8: Draft of the Main Essay Ending

When the week ended, I couldn't wait to discuss it with my business-oriented family. My mom asks me questions faster than a stockbroker. "How was it? Were you safe? Did you eat enough?" The food did not compare to hers but I mentioned how excited I was to share my finance reports. That night my family and I pour over the final finance reports from my company. My brother explains that he was learning about these financial concepts in college and my dad explains that he applied them every day at work. I feel more connected to their professions and know I took a big stride on my path to becoming a successful businessperson.

PFEW taught me about balance sheets and income statements but most importantly it made me more aware of who I can become, beyond just having a link to my family. Leaders are very important in business, but they are nothing without their team.

This ending brings the reader right back to the beginning, and it's a skillful closure of the loop.

It cannot be stressed enough that the beginning and the ending of the essay are the most important parts of the essay. Admissions Officers do not have much time to work with each student's application package so if the essay does not grab the reader from the start, then he or she might not stay with it. You really need to engage the reader from the first moment of the essay and then leave him or her with a sense of satisfaction at the end. The reader has to know a facet of your personality and perhaps understand some of your hopes and dreams for the future. He or she needs to know who you really are and perhaps who you intend to be in the future.

A good beginning has a hook that grabs the reader and alludes to the content of the essay. A good ending will tie together the story, refer back to the beginning, and leave the reader with a sense of satisfaction. Sometimes, it is good to refer to your hopes and dreams for the future in your ending. Beginnings and endings are crucial to the success of the essay.

Some of these beginnings and endings did not start out as great as they ended up, so don't worry if you're just beginning – you'll get there!

Chapter 4

Supplemental Essays

Introduction

Applying to a university via the Common App means that you only have to write one main essay, in general, but most colleges or universities require you to write one or more supplemental essays geared toward their school specifically. Even though these essays are usually short – often 250 words or less – they have to be written with utmost care. The colleges and universities pay careful attention to the responses you give because they are geared toward their individual schools.

Very often, one of the questions will be "Why do you want to go to this school?" That is a tricky one for several reasons! First of all, you can't just say, "Because it's the best!" You actually have to have a good reason, and you have to write it out. Often students are looking for a school that has a specific major, a good football team, or both. You should express that preference. That being said, you do not want to just describe what the school has. The Admissions people work there. They know what attending the school entails.

The best strategy is to go on the website of the school and find one thing that is specific to that school that you could mention in your supplemental essay.

Students who have a specific major in mind can find the specialized information that they need very easily. Students can go to the specific department website of the schools they are interested in. Most often, the department will have a faculty list that gives the research interests of each professor. Students can mention that specific professor as someone with whom they'd like to study in the future since their interests align with the professor's research. It is important to mention the academics, but it can also be useful to mention unique clubs or grants that the school offers. Ensure that the readers know you have done your research on the school and are applying purposefully.

Pro Tip:
Always always always answer the exact question asked.

Student Examples

Example 1

As I research colleges that share interests and programs I want to study for my future, I am always directed back to Indiana University's Kelly School of Business. Business is my passion and business is my life. I understand that Indiana has an amazing business program, but it has way more. When researching the school, I found that so many of the professors have interests that align with mine and I would love to study with them. One of my favorite examples is Professor Suneal Bedi and his expertise in intellectual property and marketing law and ethics. It would be a privilege to study with him and learn about the law and ethics program at Indiana. I have always had an interest in traveling and would hope to gain a position in the study abroad programs offered through the Kelly School of Business. Not only do I want to join either the Supply Chain and Operations Management Association, the Finance Investment Review organization, or the CEO at IU organization, but I would like to gain a leadership position in the organization, eventually helping to direct the work of the club. This is my prior knowledge of Indiana University, but if I have the opportunity to attend I am sure I will take advantage of the many experiences available to me.

The essay above works well because the student is able to show what he knows about the school and is able to give a specific reason why he wants to attend it. In fact, by being as detailed as he is, the student is doing a great job in demonstrating specific interests, and the Admissions Committee can see what he might do in his four years if he is admitted.

Pro Tip:
Be strong and specific in the supplemental essays. Show what you know about the school and integrate it into your interests.

Example 2

Here's another example of a shorter supplemental essay by the same student for a different business program. He was able to use some of what he wrote for Indiana University, but not all of it, since he wanted to discuss a different professor and program. It is crucial that students go over their supplemental essays with a very critical eye before submitting them. Sometimes it's tempting to use the same work, and you can copy and paste the answers. You must make sure you've changed the names and schools. Nothing is more embarrassing than gushing about a college or university and then misnaming it in your work.

I understand that the University of Wisconsin-Madison has an amazing business program, but it has way more. I would love the opportunity to discuss reconciling option prices with Professor Bjorn Eraker. The Badger Investment Banking Club and Real Estate Club all caught my eye when researching the University of Wisconsin-Madison. I have been playing Water Polo since 6th grade so the Water Polo Club at the University of Wisconsin-Madison grabbed my attention. Though I am not sure about joining, the ROTC program is a great option for me. I see myself as a great fit in the Badger Battalion.

Pro Tip:
Edit very carefully if you re-use answers to prompts. Do not mention the wrong school in an essay! Don't laugh: it happens all the time.

Example 3

Another student wanted to apply to multiple schools and had to be mindful of answering EXACTLY the question asked and not the question she wanted to answer based on what she had answered before. The first question asked, *"Why do you want to go to The University of Pittsburgh?"*

No one ever expects Japanese to come out of the mouth of a curly haired Jewish girl, but that is me. Surprisingly, in Tokyo, there is a Jewish Community. I got to have a bat-mitzvah and go to Sunday school. When I moved to the U.S, I got to explore my Judaism, and even go to Israel. University of Pittsburgh doesn't only have a strong Hillel presence, but exciting study abroad programs. That may not mean traveling back to Israel or Japan, but studying somewhere new, and possibly finding a Jewish community there.

Just like any other little girl, I wanted to be a rockstar and go to the moon, but over time, my dream job changed. Although I have always had the small dream of being a doctor, I know that is not the right path. At Pittsburgh, I can be a Health Management major and learn about organization of data, helping me to one day run a hospital on the analytical or management side. It would be an honor to study with Professor Kevin D Broom, an award winning Health Management professor.

Not only does the University of Pittsburgh have great Major options, but interesting minors as well. Growing up in Japan I learned the language, and immersed myself in the culture. At Pittsburgh, they don't only offer a major in Japanese, but a minor as well. This will give me the opportunity to continue my Japanese and deepen my language skills. Having researched the program, and learning about the professors, it would be in honor to study under Professor Hiroshi Nara. It is always a great opportunity to learn from a native speaker. After not living in Japan for a few years now, I always love connecting with other Japanese people who have lived there and enjoy the language.

Not only the academics but the opportunities to learn and grow as a student makes my desire to go to Pittsburgh increase [sic]. Coming from a big football family, football has always been a part of my childhood. Watching football games on Saturdays with my dad is a fond memory. Pittsburgh has a great football team with lots of school spirit, and that is something I look for in a school. I can't wait for the day for my dad to come and visit me and go to a game together.

The University of Pittsburgh is the place for me because it has Judaism, Japanese, my dream job, school spirit, and football. I can not wait to be a panther.

This student's essay is strong, creative, and answers the question asked in multiple ways. She was able to use the bare bones of this work in other schools' supplemental essays but had to be very careful and mindful about what actual school information goes where. In the end, the work of being mindful here will pay off.

?
> **Question for you:**
> *What is the difference between asking why you want to go to a school and what will you bring to a school? They are inherently different; think about how and why.*

Example 4

This is a part of the same student's essay, modified to fit a similar prompt from the University of Wisconsin at Madison, where the question was "What excites you about going to the University of Wisconsin?":

At Wisconsin, I can be a statistics major and learn all about organization of data helping me one day be able to run a hospital on the analytical or management side. One of the University's award winning professors, Rick Chappell, doesn't only teach statistics, but medical informatics, my dream job. Learning from him and all the talented faculty at University of Wisconsin Madison will only deepen my love for health data science and bring me closer to my dream job. This major could lead me to work in a hospital without being a doctor, but still be an important body, achieving the goal I have always wanted.

Not only does University of Wisconsin Madison have great Major options, but interesting minors as well. Growing up in Japan I learned the language, and immersed myself in the culture. At UWM, they don't only offer a major in Japanese, but a minor as well. This will give me the opportunity to continue my Japanese and deepen my language skills. Having researched the program, and learning about the professors, it would be an honor to study under Professor Naomi Fujita Geyer. It is always a great opportunity to learn from a native speaker. After not living in Japan for a few years now, I always love connecting with other Japanese people who have lived there and enjoy the language.

Not only the academics but the opportunities to learn and grow as a student makes my desire to go to UWM increase. Coming from a Big 10 family, football has always been a part of my childhood. Watching football games on Saturdays with my dad is a fond memory. UWM has a great football team with lots of school spirit, and that is something I look for in a school. I can't wait for the day for my dad to come and visit me and go to a game together.

Look at the two essays above. How are they the same? How are they different?

Please note that the question from The University of Wisconsin was "What excites you?" while the one from the University of Pittsburgh was "Why us?" Always remember to use language geared toward answering precisely the question asked.

Example 5 - Re-using a Supplemental Essay

Sometimes it's possible to modify essays for different uses. If you are applying to an Honors College of a college or university (watch the deadlines on those, by the way – they're often early!) they will likely require a separate essay with a strong and specific question.

Here's a supplemental essay, with the question, one student wrote to get into a prestigious Honors College:

The art we see, the stories we read, and the words we hear have the power to move us and to change us. Tell us about a time that you've been moved to act by something you read, a speech you heard, or a work of art that you experienced. What was it, and how did it impact you? What did you do -- or what will you do -- in response? (500 words)

The first time I was truly moved by a book I was in elementary school. I believe it was 5th grade and I read a book called **A Monster Calls**. I had to read a book for some project and I didn't want to do it so I put it off until the last minute and read the entire book in one night. I don't consider myself a very emotional person but that was the first time that, after experiencing a piece of media, I cried real full tears. Sure, I had shed the occasional tear at a sad scene in a movie, but that was the first time in my 10 years of life that a story made me break down and truly think about what the story meant. **A Monster Calls** is about a boy whose mother has cancer, and a monster helps him through it, and tries to help him save his mother. What shook me was when it was revealed that there was no monster, and it was his inner desires that he was imagining the entire time as a way to cope. At this point in my life, I had never experienced media that had a deeper meaning, and it really made me look at my own life from a different perspective. It made me realize that life is fragile, and if I don't take action on things, I might get left behind.

I never truly related to the book until my sophomore year when I lost both my aunt and grandfather in the same weekend, and for the first time in my life I was put in the place of the main character. I thought about the book a lot during the following month, but I never read it for fear of crying. I didn't need to read the book again to know what I should do in the situation I was in; I needed to move on. The difference between me and the main character of the book was that I didn't get to go on a fantastical adventure, I was only stuck with my grief.

In the end I did end up reading the book again, and crying when I finished. Reading the book again, having it fresh in my mind did help me move on. However, it wasn't just reading the content of the book that helped me move on; it was knowing that millions of other people had done the same in my situation, and that they pushed forward for the legacy of the ones they lost. It was the most valuable lesson I ever got from a book. Life will throw punches and all you can do is work through it and look forward to a brighter future. I know my aunt and grandfather would be proud of me taking steps toward my future.

Example 6 - Re-using Example 5

Another one of the universities this same student was applying to asked him the following question: **Explain how a book you read helped you understand the world's complexity. (150 words)**

Look carefully below: the student was then able to take the main ideas from his Honors College essay from one application (see above) and modify it down to the following supplemental essay. See if you can notice the differences and similarities.

*When I read **A Monster Call**s I didn't understand its true meaning. I was 10 and had never lost anyone before, but even still I cried after reading it. It was the first time a loss had been thrust before me. I would often think back to the book when dozing in school. It was almost a habit to think about what the book meant to me.*

A few years ago my grandpa and aunt died in one week, and I truly understood the meaning of the book. Thinking back on it, the book truly gave me an understanding of what it would be like to lose someone. It gave me a taste of horrible feelings that no one should ever have to go through. I learned of how powerful books could be in that moment, and it gives me an appreciation for every other book I read.

The essay went from 500 words to 150! By distilling it down to the major points, the student was able to re-purpose work already done, but it had to be done carefully so as not to go over the word count or reference a school other than the one to which he was applying.

Pro Tip:

It's great to reuse essay fodder. Just be careful and intentional when doing so. Edit carefully!

Short Supplemental Questions and Answers

Some places, like the University of Maryland (UMD), want to see what you can do so they ask questions and require short, pithy answers that are under 100 words. Here's an example of the set of UMD questions and answers from one student a few years ago:

If I could travel anywhere, I would go to...*

Israel because of my family and deep faith. Through my family's commitment to hosting foreign exchange students, I have made many friends who live there.

The most interesting fact I ever learned from the research was...*

That, according to Neil Degrasse Tyson, the first trillionaire not due to inflation will be the first person to start asteroid mining.

In addition to my major, my academic interests include...*

Astronomy and biology. I hope to leave this atmosphere one day.

My favorite thing about last Tuesday was...*

I scored my first goal against our rival team in my water polo game. I have been trained as a goalie but wanted to try the field positions.

Something you might not know about me is...*

I am fascinated by the movie world and would like to be a part of the film industry someday.

The University of Maryland's application process literally wants students to write like in Twitter – using 140 characters. How might you answer these questions? Can you stay within the 140-character limit?

Examples of Really Great Supplemental Questions and Answers from Various Schools

If you could change one thing about where you live, what would it be and why? (200-250 words)

One small latte, a double macchiato, and a medium cold brew. These are just a few of my many regulars' drinks at Greenberry's. Among all of my regulars, I have realized a common occurrence. I like to call it "The morning panic." Day in and day out, each customer comes at their usual morning time with a look of panic on their face. Many of them wake up at 5 a.m., go to the gym next door, come to get their coffee, and drive an hour to work in the D.C. traffic. Always moving, and always running behind. I squeeze in a "Good morning" but I rarely get a response. Their minds are like printers that are already overheating at the idea of printing their first sheet. Jerry comes in every morning wearing head to toe scrubs, talking on the phone, and spilling his cash onto the counter. As I rummaged through the register, almost breaking a sweat, I wished that everything could just pause. Before living in Virginia, I had lived in a small town in Pennsylvania. There, if I had said my usual "Good morning", I would have gotten a response that started with small talk, and ended with their life story. With a slower paced lifestyle, I could connect with the people around me. Here, I see these people every day, and I know nothing about them. Although neither of these extremes is favorable, I hope to one day reach a medium of both worlds.

. . . .

To notice above:
Details details details - she SHOWS you the scenes but does very little telling. How might you show a scene at a store?

. . . .

Describe someone who you see as a community builder. What actions has that person taken? How has their work made a difference in your life? (200-250 words)

It's 8:00 a.m. Just like every other morning, he is standing at the door of the choir room singing "Here's your note" in the key of the sight reading for that day. He is known by his students as "Doc": a seemingly stern choral director with a distinctly powerful presence. He directs with meticulous attention to detail and a trained ear that can distinguish one wrong vowel amongst a stage of singers. While he has built a choir community through his many choir events and concerts, I believe that his key to single-handedly building the choir community comes down to one simple tool — the choir room. Although other teachers' classrooms are just for class, Doc's classroom is a multifunctional space for all 65 of his choir students. Before-school power naps and free period study sessions in the choir room are a common sight. The music notes written on the whiteboard are constantly erased and replaced with calculus homework problems. The word "Cafeteria" is almost unknown to his students as we always feast in the choir room. Since he allows his room to stay unlocked and double as a second home, his students always have a safe place to go. In my eyes, a community builder doesn't have to be someone who is world renowned or has affected thousands of people. The community that has provided me with my best memories and friends simply began with one director and his open doors.

To notice above:
We can "see" the room the student describes but we also get a feeling about it. What words in the brief essay make you feel something about the room?

Engineering is inherently collaborative. What does collaboration mean to you? What strengths do you bring to the collaborative process? (150 words)

Collaboration, to me, means an exchange of ideas and solutions. When collaborating with others, I find that my strength lies in taking in and combining all the ideas that others have. I am a great listener and I can assess the ideas of others quite well. For example during this year's robotics club, I asked everyone for ideas on how to get a ball up off of the ground and into a secured location. Most of the ideas revolved around a claw, but they all were all impractical. Since they were mostly inexperienced, I pointed this out to them and tried to lead them in the right direction. In the end our design was better than anything they came up with alone, and it was better then what I could have done alone.

To notice above:
The student is not writing a definition of collaboration but rather specifically, how he handles collaboration. Can you see the difference between those two ideas? In the latter, the student is the main idea of the essay, not the collaboration itself.

The University of Miami's official mascot is the ibis. Folklore maintains that the native marsh bird is the last to take shelter before a hurricane hits and the first to emerge once the storm passes, making it an apt symbol of courage and resilience. Considering your ability to control your own motivation and behavior, how have past experiences helped build your courage and resilience to persist in the face of academic and life challenges so that, once these storms pass, you can emerge in continued pursuit of your goals? (250 words)

Growing up in Japan, sheltered by small private schools, made the transition to a public school in the U.S difficult. In my class of fifty students with a six-to-one teacher ratio, someone always watched over me. If I received a bad grade or acted upset in class, I had no worry that a teacher would help. When I moved back to the U.S in seventh grade, my class of fifty became 400, increasing to 500 in High School. Not only was I transitioning to an American High School, but also a larger class size. Whether it was writing an essay, or doing math homework, everything was harder. I knew I was struggling, but I was confused why teachers hadn't reached out. This is when I learned I had to take the initiative to talk to teachers. Although it seems simple to walk up to a teacher and ask for simple instruction, I had never done this before. Working up the courage to ask for help from a teacher was my first step in succeeding. Eventually, I gained the courage and asked my math teacher for help. Of course she was willing, and I only benefited from it. From then on, I looked to my teachers to be resources. Looking back today, I couldn't imagine what I was scared of. That simple act has only exemplified my work as a student, and I plan on continuing in college. Asking for help never hurts.

· ·

To notice above:

the student mentions a problem, but more than half of the short essay is spent on how she overcame it. Thus, she appears resilient and creative.

· ·

Supplemental essays are varied in their topics. Some schools want long ones and some schools want short ones. Some schools don't have any. Please be sure to read the application for each school carefully well ahead of the deadlines so you know what you have to do specifically for each school and what the deadline really is. Some people find it very helpful to put together a spreadsheet of main essays and supplemental essays they have to do so they are certain nothing gets lost. Whatever you do, answer the question asked to the fullest of your ability.

Really great supplemental essays let the readers know you are specifically interested in the specific school. While the prompt for the main essay is very flexible, in the case of supplemental essays, it is crucial to always answer the question asked as specifically as you can.

Chapter 5

The COVID-19 Prompt

In June 2020, the Common App website (www.commonapp.org) announced that it would have a separate, short-answer question for students to answer regarding the Coronavirus and its effects. In the years since then, it has remained a fixture on the Common Application. If you are looking for it, it's not located in the same area of the website as the regular essay submissions, nor is it with the supplemental essays, but rather located in the "additional information" section.

The extra prompt is meant for students who need to explain something about their experience of the virus and the way it affected them. It is completely optional and meant for those whose lives were upended in various ways. It's not a place, for example, to tell about how you staved off boredom by making masks when you were stuck at home for months on end. It's a very short piece – a box with only 250 words allowed at the most. Before you decide you need to address the prompt, consider the reason why you want to do it.

If you decide to address the question, please make sure to answer the question asked. It's not about what you *did* during the virus; it's about how the virus had ripple effects on your life and the way you live it, which might very well have interrupted your schooling, so an explanation would be prudent.

The COVID-19 Prompt - Examples

The prompt itself gives a few examples of what you might need or want to disclose. A few more specific examples include:

- If your parent lost his or her job and the effect that had on you.
- The loss of any direct caregiver to the virus – parent, step-parent, or close grandparent.
- If you had to move as a result of the virus affecting your family.
- If you had to become a caregiver to anyone in your family for any reason as a result of the pandemic.

Be very sure to focus on the effect the change had on YOU, and not just what happened. The inclination of most students would be to describe the event and what happened and then let the reader think about how terrible it was. It is not clear how individual schools are looking at this prompt several years after the beginning of the virus, but it is still being included in the application.

The COVID-19 Prompt from the Common App Website

COVID-19 has affected students in dramatically different ways. If you need it, the COVID-19 and natural disaster question in the Additional Information section is a place for you to describe the impact of these events.

The question is not intended to be an extra essay. There's also no need to describe how your school responded to these events. Your counselor will have an opportunity to discuss impacts like closures, online instruction, and grading policies. Instead, consider how these events may have impacted you, your family, and your learning environment. Examples might include:

You do not have to address the COVID-19 prompt. It is optional. If you do not have a compelling story to tell about the effects of the pandemic, then it is okay to leave it blank.

- Illness or loss within your family or support network

- Employment or housing disruptions within your family

- Food insecurity

- Toll on mental and emotional health

- New obligations such as part-time work or care for siblings or family members

- Availability of computer or internet access required to continue your studies

- Access to a safe and quiet study space

- A new direction for your major or career interests
  (Commonapp.org)

Examples of Responses to the COVID-19 Prompt

Example #1:

One student used it to explain some gaps in his otherwise stellar grade point average.

During the Pandemic, my school went fully online and then changed to a hybrid model. In addition, my school implemented a new grading method. Online learning was very hard for students like me, with ADHD. Trying to adapt to the new circumstances, my grades suffered heavily. Furthermore, My health was impacted in two ways. I had major surgery at the beginning of the school year and later on, I contracted the Covid-19 virus. This really affected my studies because attending virtual classes while sick or recovering from surgery caused a gap in learning before I took major subject tests. My family all contracted the virus which created further stress.

Example #2:

Another student used the space to show that she learned a lot about helping others through the pandemic lockdowns.

"Now let's pick up the quarter cup, and scoop one quarter cup of flour and put it into the bowl."

As the Corona virus hit and my Junior year came to an end, the world felt like a very dark place. Luckily there is one activity that always brings me joy: Cooking/Baking.

I started cooking up a storm, making Indonesian fried rice, challah, cakes, muffins and so much more. My mother was so impressed with all my creations that she started posting them on Facebook. One day an old friend of hers messaged her and asked if I would be interested in making a cooking video for special needs kids that she taught. When I heard the news I was so excited. I learned that due to the corona virus and schools closing, special needs kids were getting the least help with school work and activities.

I could use my love of cooking to help others, so I started making basic cooking videos that were then shared with special needs kids, so they could make basic foods like brownies without too much outside instruction.

Then I started giving online cooking lessons to my cousin with Down Syndrome as well. We practiced basic things like measuring out flour to help her get confident in baking. My work with my cousin has continued through the school year. I am grateful that my family remained healthy and protected during this time, and that I got to help others in the process.

It is not at all required that you respond to the COVID-19 prompt, and in fact, as the pandemic eases in many places, the severity and the lockdowns have eased as well, so the question is less pertinent to the current moment in time. If you do not have something very specific and relevant to say, I'd suggest leaving the space devoted to the prompt blank.

This page is intentionally left blank

Chapter 6

Some Things Just Don't Fit the Mold

There are a few schools that have very interesting supplemental essay questions that are outside of the range of normal questions, and then there are a few schools that are not on the Common App at all and have their own application portals. This chapter will address both types of anomalies and how you might approach them.

Part I: Supplemental Essay Questions that are Outside of the Range of Normal Questions

Example 1: Wake Forest University

Some schools, such as Wake Forest University in North Carolina, ask for a list of some sort. The application web page of this school states that the following questions are optional, but most college counselors would tell you to always address optional questions if you can. Here are the 2022 optional application questions/requests from Wake Forest University.

1. List five books you've read that have intrigued you.

2. Explain how a text you've read – fiction, nonfiction, poetry, or literature of any kind – has helped you understand the world's complexity (limit 150 words).

3. What piques your intellectual curiosity and why (limit 150 words)?

4. Give us your Top Ten list (The choice of theme is yours) (limit 100 characters per line).

There are several ideas to keep in mind here. Beyond just addressing the questions/prompts, you must follow the instructions exactly. The book list should simply be a list of titles. The word limits on the prompts are very specific. They do not want you to explain each item on your Top Ten list; just give the list. All these things should be representative of YOU and your ideas and thoughts.

Pro Tip:
Always always always answer the exact question asked!

Some students wonder if the list of five texts in Prompt 1 should match the question of how a text has affected them. The answer is, of course, perhaps. It depends on whether you are a strong or interested reader. You do have to address both prompts but you should also always be honest. If a book has affected you enough to write about it, then definitely do, but if you want to discuss some other type of text, then please go with that. The school and the Admissions Committee want to connect with you and it is best to give them a sense of who you are and what you think about in the most truthful way possible.

Perhaps you are a sports fan. You might want to give a Top Ten list of your favorite football plays. That's fine as long as you're succinct. Doing something like a list of plays might sound cliché, but it does show that you're not just any sports fan; you're a sports fan with an eye for detail. Maybe you are a foodie and want to give a list of your favorite restaurants and each one's signature dish. That also shows an eye for detail and also discerning taste. It still, no matter what, cannot exceed 100 characters per line of the list.

The intellectual curiosity question is an intriguing possibility. It might be related to your choice of major, but it doesn't have to be.

One student I met answered that question with something unrelated but highly philosophical: Why can't people agree on conventional grammar standards in an international language such as English? She had recently come across the idea of linguistic justice, in which language is not only cultural, but personal, and the concept captured her imagination because she wants to go into the practice of law. Who is to say what speaking the "right" way is, she asks? This is the perfect idea to show the Admissions Committee at Wake Forest University something that has engaged her imagination.

Pro Tip:
It's okay - good, even - to be creative in a small way. If the school is asking creative questions, you have a little bit of creative license.

Other responses to that question have been about black holes in space, gene editing, artificial intelligence, or other things that just generally interest young people. This prompt is similar to one you might get at any other college or university but in conjunction with the other prompts, it makes for some interesting reading and writing.

Sample Response to Prompt 4

My Top Ten Favorite Holiday Traditions:

1. *Eating Grandma's brisket: in a word, YUM.*
2. *Driving over the George Washington bridge to Grandma's house.*
3. *Father's Day swimming at Auntie's house.*
4. *Watching the fancy ladies in synagogue on Rosh Hashanah.*
5. *Teaching my friends to light a menorah.*
6. *Mom bringing matzah and jam to my classrooms.*
7. *Going to Grammy's in Florida for winter break.*
8. *Seeing palm trees with Christmas lights.*
9. *Scheming with my brother for Hanukkah gifts for our parents.*
10. *The feelings of warmth, light, and love always.*

This list says quite a bit about the student. It shows that he is family-oriented, notices details, and has warm memories of growing up. It says that he is Jewish, and not only follows traditions but looks to share them with others. Those are just some of the details that any Admissions Committee will glean from his list. Please note that the requirement for Prompt 4 says that each line cannot contain more than 100 characters. The lines of this list are all short but have been carefully checked. Even if you feel the need to explain items on your list, you must keep each line at or under 100 characters.

. . . .

To note above:
What words above make you feel like you know this student in a limited way? What can you glean about him from each item in the top ten? What does your top ten look like?

. . . .

Sample Response to Prompt 1

Five books that have intrigued me:

1. *Beloved by Toni Morrison*
2. *Extremely Loud and Incredibly Close by Jonathan Safran Foer*
3. *The Book Thief by Marcus Zusak*
4. *To Kill a Mockingbird by Harper Lee*
5. *The Curious Incident of the Dog in the Night-Time by Mark Haddon*

Remember, with your list, you can only give the title and author. Let the Admissions Committee infer what they will from your compilation. Be strong and honest and show them that you have read a variety of texts. It is okay if some of them were for school and it's okay if not all of them are fiction, as this student has given.

* *

To note above:

This is a great exercise to just practice with as you prepare to write. What are your favorite books? If you just list them, what do they say about you?

* *

Sample Response to the "Text that Affects" question that relates to the list

My parents gave me the book The Curious Incident of the Dog in the Night-Time when I was fourteen and my brother James was seventeen. James and I are very different. For example, James reads all the time and is a gifted musician. He can sit and play his guitar, horn, or piano for hours while I'm always out with my buddies. The book is written from the point of view of a boy who is similar to my brother, on the Autism spectrum. The book helped me understand some of the ways my brother might think or look at the world. Before reading this book, I didn't have ways to relate to my brother. But afterward, I found ways to talk to him not only about the things he likes, but am now able to help him understand the things that I like and think about. I also learned that there is power in literature.

Whatever choice you make, just be sure to be clear and honest in all aspects of your work and always answer the question asked.

This student does a great job of explaining how one of the books on his list made an impression on him and why that is the case. However, I have seen many versions of this essay where the book described is not on the list. The two prompts do have different wording. Prompt 1 asks for books that have intrigued a student while the explanation prompt asks for books that have changed the student's worldview in some way. Those two things can be linked but they do not have to be.

Example 2: Innovative Prompts

There are many other schools that ask for a list of some sort, either with or without explanation. Some universities have other really unique prompts like the University of Pennsylvania's perennial question: "You have just finished your 300-page autobiography. Please submit page 217." One year Tufts University had a prompt that said something along the lines of "Kermit the Frog famously laments that it's not easy being green. Do you agree or disagree?" Other schools do have supplemental essay questions that might seem a little crazy, but you still have to address them and do it creatively, with your own ideas and voice. It's okay to be "out there" and quite creative with these questions, as long as you are within the bounds of reason. Rely on family and friends to help you if needed with drafting and revising.

Example 3: The University of Chicago

The school with the most innovative, creative, and daring prompts is definitely The University of Chicago. Its first prompt is pretty regular, similar to many schools' supplemental essay prompts: "How does The University of Chicago, as you know it now, satisfy your desire for a particular kind of learning, community, and future? Please address with some specificity your own wishes and how they relate to The University of Chicago" This question is written in a particular way, with the knowledge that you have not yet been to the university, so you only have an outsider's perspective on it – hence the words "as you know it now." Additionally, many schools ask why you want to go there, what you will do at that school, or what you hope to get out of going to that school. This prompt specifically asks how The University of Chicago will "satisfy your desire for a particular type of learning." You must discuss the educational experience in various ways but always relate it back to learning. Even if you want to talk about how you have always wanted to live in the city of Chicago, you have to relate it back to learning somehow; perhaps mentioning how the city will be part of your classroom.

....

To note:
The University of Chicago is a highly selective school. Answering these questions creatively and thoughtfully takes a good deal of thought and work. The Admissions Committee clearly values those aspects of a student.

....

Every year, The University of Chicago's second supplemental essay requirements get more and more interesting and the university asks its students to weigh in on what the applicants should write, so on its website/application you will see who "inspired" the question and what year he or she either graduated or will graduate from the university. Here are the 2022-2023 prompts:

Question 2: Extended Essay (Required; Choose one)

Essay Option 1

Was it a cat I saw? Yo-no-na-ka, ho-ka-ho-ka na-no-yo (Japanese for "the world is a warm place"). Może jutro ta dama da tortu jeżom (Polish for "maybe tomorrow that lady will give a cake to the hedgehogs"). Share a palindrome in any language, and give it a backstory.
- *Inspired by Leah Beach, Class of 2026, Lib Gray SB '12, and Agnes Mazur AB '09*

Essay Option 2

What advice would a wisdom tooth have?
—*Inspired by Melody Dias, Class of 2025*

Essay Option 3

You are on an expedition to found a colony on Mars, when from a nearby crater, a group of Martians suddenly emerges. They seem eager to communicate, but they're the impatient kind and demand you represent the human race in one song, image, memory, proof, or other idea. What do you share with them to show that humanity is worth their time?

—*Inspired by Alexander Hastings, Class of 2023, and Olivia Okun-Dubitsky, Class of 2026*

Essay Option 4

The University of Chicago has been affiliated with over 90 Nobel laureates. But, why should economics, physics, and peace get all the glory? You are tasked with creating a new category for the Nobel Prize. Explain what it would be, why you chose your specific category, and the criteria necessary to achieve this accomplishment.

—*Inspired by Isabel Alvarez, Class of 2026*

Essay Option 5

Genghis Khan with an F1 race car. George Washington with a SuperSoaker. Emperor Nero with a toaster. Leonardo da Vinci with a Furby. If you could give any historical figure any piece of technology, who and what would it be, and why do you think they'd work so well together?

-*Inspired by Braden Hajer, Class of 2025*

Essay Option 6

And, as always… the classic choose your own adventure option! In the spirit of adventurous inquiry, choose one of our past prompts (or create a question of your own). Be original, creative, and thought-provoking. Draw on your best qualities as a writer, thinker, visionary, social critic, sage, a citizen of the world, or future citizen of The University of Chicago; take a little risk, and have fun!

The University of Chicago's website lists prompts like these but also lists many from prior years as well. You can feel free to choose one of the prompts from a prior year to answer instead of the new ones listed.

A 2021 news story from the University's own news site mentions that the creative extended essay prompts "encourage applicants to think beyond traditional Admissions essay conventions and freely express themselves" (https://news.uchicago.edu/story/unique-uchicago-essay-questions-spark-students-creativity). The story goes on to add that the Admissions Committee can see not only creativity but problem-solving skills in the essay responses. Inevitably, students run into situations in college that they have never encountered before and the University feels that answering these deep and varied questions allows the Admissions Committee to see who will respond well to the pressures of life at The University of Chicago.

You will note that neither of the essay prompts from The University of Chicago has word limits listed. They rely on your best judgment to write until you are done without going overboard. Sometimes NOT having a word limit can be challenging for students because it allows for a bit of rambling. In addition, without a word count, students often do not check their essays for conciseness, making sure that every word written is important enough to be included in the essay. Please always revise and edit your work carefully.

Pro Tip:
Use your best judgment on which prompts to answer and at what length.

It bears repeating that whatever supplemental essay prompts that the universities to which you are applying utilize, you must always answer the question asked specifically and revise your work carefully to make it strong, concise, and representative of who you are.

Part II. NOT on the Common or Coalition App

The following section discusses large and popular universities in the U.S. that have their own application process and do not subscribe to the Common or Coalition Application sites. This is not an exhaustive list, but rather a sampling. You must always check to see if the school to which you are applying accepts the Common App or if it has its own application portal. All of the following schools have their own application portal on their websites.

Example 1: The University of California

The University of California has nine campuses across the state and has one application portal for all of them. It does not use the Common App website or forms at all. Students must submit all materials, including their essay prompts, via The University of California portal directly. The University of California calls its essays "Personal Insight Questions" and the school gives you eight prompts, out of which you must choose four. You may only write 350 words per prompt at the most. The prompts are not that different from supplemental essays for other colleges and universities, but bear in mind that the Admissions Committee for The University of California will not see your main essay; they only have access to the answers to these prompts.

Each prompt is listed on The University of California's website and gives some things to consider for each one so that students can feel guided and less confused. The prompts for 2022-2023 are as follows:

1. Describe an example of your leadership experience in which you have positively influenced others, helped resolve disputes, or contributed to group efforts over time.

2. Every person has a creative side, and it can be expressed in many ways: problem-solving, original and innovative thinking, and artistically, to name a few. Describe how you express your creative side.

3. What would you say is your greatest talent or skill? How have you developed and demonstrated that talent over time?

4. Describe how you have taken advantage of a significant educational opportunity or worked to overcome an educational barrier you have faced.

5. Describe the most significant challenge you have faced and the steps you have taken to overcome this challenge. How has this challenge affected your academic achievement?

6. Think about an academic subject that inspires you. Describe how you have furthered this interest inside and/or outside of the classroom.

7. What have you done to make your school or your community a better place?

8. Beyond what has already been shared in your application, what do you believe makes you a strong candidate for admission to The University of California?

As mentioned, for each question here, the website (admission. univesityofcalifornia.edu) lists a few guiding questions below it. For example, underneath the second question about your creative side, the website asks not only how you express it, but if you want to discuss how it might influence your decisions both inside and outside of the classroom.

☞ **Reminder:**
Every question has a purpose. Before answering a question, think of what the Admissions Committee might want to know exactly.

The question about challenges reminds you to stay focused on how you overcame the challenge and not only discuss what the challenge actually is. The question about making your community a better place asks you what inspired you to do what you did, so you're not only discussing what happened, but how it happened, why it happened, and what it means in the context of your life and college application. This is the art of true reflection. The Admissions Committee is looking not only for a discussion of the events of the question but also for evidence of self-awareness and ultimately, self-reflection. Do you understand yourself? Can you talk to others about what you understand about yourself? These questions are important to master and understand.

As a reminder, the website explicitly tells students that these essays are only one piece of the puzzle of Admissions and the answers to these questions are not the main way to evaluate Admissions decisions for The University of California. Students are advised to do their best work but also to write, edit, solicit feedback, and most of all, try to relax – advice that is important and great, but also hard to follow!

Example 2: Massachusetts Institute of Technology (MIT)

MIT is one of the most prestigious universities in the U.S. and is highly selective in its Admissions decisions. It is also one of the few notable schools that do not use the Common App website. MIT, like The University of California, has its own Admissions portal. The MIT questions/essay prompts, however, are fewer and shorter. You must answer all of the questions in approximately 200 words each and there is a text box in which you can add some important information if there is something you were not able to address with the prompts given and the school really needs to know it. This is something you do not need to do unless you have some special situation that MIT should understand when reading your application. You do not need to put anything in the box if there is not some extenuating circumstance that you want to address.

Remember, the school will NOT see the main essay that you wrote for the Common App website, so if there is interesting or unique information or stories in that essay, then perhaps you can break it up or even shorten parts of it for use on the MIT website.

MIT's 2022-2023 Prompts:

1. We know you lead a busy life, full of activities, many of which are required of you. Tell us about something you do simply for the pleasure of it.

2. Describe the world you come from (for example, your family, school, community, city, or town). How has that world shaped your dreams and aspirations?

3. MIT brings people with diverse backgrounds and experiences together to better the lives of others. Our students work to improve

their communities in different ways, from tackling the world's biggest challenges to being a good friend. Describe one way you have collaborated with people who are different from you to contribute to your community.

4. Tell us about a significant challenge you've faced (that you feel comfortable sharing) or something that didn't go according to plan. How did you manage the situation?

Pro Tip:

Follow the instructions very very carefully. If you do not do exactly as required, the Admissions Committees may not read your work fully or even at all.

The instructions here are very specific. You must answer all the questions and you must do it in a short amount of words. Think about the brainstorming prompts we used in the first part of this book; some of these are similar prompts but you cannot use them together. I have worked with several students who have applied to MIT and they often try to get parts of their main essays into the short answer responses, but I always remind them to specifically answer the question asked. For example, I had a student who wrote his main essay for the Common App about being first-generation American; his parents were from India. A small part of that went into the question about the world he came from and how it has shaped him. Some of his other responses to MIT were somewhat lifted from that essay as well.

Here's one good example:

My family is Muslim and we worship at a mosque nearby. In my Junior year, a Rabbi from a local synagogue approached our youth group about working with their teen youth. Together we planned an afterschool homework help program at an elementary school that had many kids who needed assistance. It took us a lot of meetings to plan the program and we started every meeting with an icebreaker so we could get to know each other on a deeper level.

Eventually we started and it went smoothly. We had three different teens in the elementary school three times a week and we ensured there was a mix of teens there. The young kids were happy to see us! Our two teen groups continued to meet monthly to make tweaks to the program. Everyone was pleased with our work.

It was a great way for youth in our community to come together to help other youth and we got to know each other in a way we would not have. Our main lesson was that we are more alike than different. I will carry that with me in every group context I find myself in, I just know it.

The essay above is a shortened version of his Common App Essay modified for use for MIT. That, together with the short essay about being from an Indian family, will give MIT a fuller picture of who the student is, which is the point of the exercise here. The other two pieces the student wrote were about the joy of riding a bicycle, both for pleasure and as a mode of transportation, and the challenge of bringing lunch to school when he was younger because his mother insisted on packing him Indian food, which was unfamiliar to his classmates. Those two ideas also added a lot to the picture of the student.

👉 **Reminder:**
Even these short essays are designed so that the Admissions Committee can get to know who you are. Think carefully again about what you want them to know about you, your values, and what you stand for.

Example 3: Georgetown University

Applying to Georgetown University in Washington D.C. is a very specific process. You have to fill out a quick set of forms that stimulates an account creation on the school's end and only then you will get access to the rest of the application, including the essay prompts.

The prompts themselves are not that different from those of other schools, but it is again worth noting that since the school will not see your main essay like other schools that accept the Common App, you might want to sneak in part of that essay if it highlights a particular part of your personality or uniqueness if you can. Here are sample Georgetown University prompts:

Prompt #1: Indicate any special talents or skills you possess. (250 words)

Prompt #2: Briefly discuss the significance to you of the school or summer activity in which you have been most involved. (approximately 1/2 page, single-spaced)

Prompt #3: As Georgetown University is a diverse community, the Admissions Committee would like to know more about you in your own words. Submit a brief essay, either personal or creative, which you feel best describes you. (approximately 1 page, single-spaced)

These prompts are not only specific but also require you to adhere to a specific word or page count strictly. Part of the process is how well you follow directions, clearly.

In addition to these specific prompts that all applicants answer, Georgetown University has a prompt that students must address for each college in the university they apply to. Students apply to a school when they apply to Georgetown University, not just to the university as a whole, and the prompt for each school is different. For example, the prompt for the School of Nursing and Health Studies asks you what influenced your decision to apply into a healthcare field, and the prompt for the School of Business wants to know what influenced your decision to study business, specifically at Georgetown University.

The famous Georgetown School of Foreign Service has a very strong prompt that must be addressed carefully: "The Walsh School of Foreign Service was founded more than a century ago to prepare generations of leaders to solve global problems. What is motivating you to dedicate your undergraduate studies to a future in service to the world?" The question assumes you will dedicate your life to service if you study there, so your answer needs to address that probability.

Pro Tip:

For highly selective schools that are not on the Common App, be sure to put your best foot forward and answer each question precisely and honestly. .

No matter what the supplemental prompt asks or if the school is on the Common App or not, keep in mind that the short answer essays, like your main essay, are just one piece of the Admissions puzzle, and grades, rigor, and recommendations are still very important, but doing your best on the essays and answering the questions exactly as asked are crucial parts as well.

Chapter 7

Example Essays

This chapter contains sample essays from students. Each essay has an opening comment including a specific idea of what makes it work. Please keep in mind that these essays have all been through many drafts and the students who wrote them agonized over them for weeks, if not months. Sometimes looking at completed essays can be daunting if you're in the brainstorming phase – you're comparing your ideas to a finished ideal essay, and it's scary. But if you work on your essay as much as these eleven students worked on theirs, then you too will produce an essay that is representative of you and your personality. Keep writing and writing and revising and revising – you'll get there!

All included essays are used with permission, but anonymously.

Essay #1: A Story About a Religious "Home"

Effort, Gratification, Compassion

As dawn breaks, I pull open a heavy, wooden door and walk down the stone floor of a dim hallway. The sound of steel and glass clinking together on a wobbling cart rolling through each hallway is one of the only sounds in a calm, quiet church. Another thick door swings open, and a bright light instantly illuminates a small kitchen. An assortment of bread is sorted onto a beautiful, shining silver dish and grape juice is squeezed into tiny clear glasses the size of one's palm. I fill the stone goblets with more grape juice and I place a giant bread loaf onto another illustrious plate. These items crowd the cart as it wobbles into a massive, bright sanctuary filled with the angelic voices of the choir. I carefully assort this army of dishes and plates onto a table. I step back down the stoned floor and look up at the stained glass with Jesus looking down onto the table, feeling like I have accomplished something. Communion is ready for serving. Since first grade, I have done this bimonthly.

Preparing communion is not the only activity I have participated in at church. The congregation took notice of my effort, work and involvement. Two years ago they appointed me to be the youth elder on the Session, the church's governing board. Serving as youth elder is an honor for me because I am serving the congregation. Adrenaline rushes into me every time I walk into the monthly meetings because I feel obligated to speak up for those in the congregation who are unable to be heard and strive to make the church a better place. For example, improving church safety and making plans to prevent mass shootings are things I consistently advocate for even when unease fills the room at the mention of the topics. As the only student present on Session, being around adults is something I learn from and enjoy. Persevering, working hard and being compassionate to others are things they taught me. Persistently advocating for issues during Session meetings, working hard to fix them and being positive have contributed to my maturity due to those interactions.

These experiences at church have prepared me for life outside of it as well. I am known for having a calm, kind and empathetic personality. Many people have come to me for help or advice, something that is a privilege because not everyone gains that level of trust. I remember sitting in a small group with a school counselor in a cozy, small room when someone shared a rough experience at home. I calmly spoke to her about it and tried to give her advice about what to do. For a while I remember the student consistently thanking me, because the advice I gave eased her situation. I am glad I impacted someone's life in that way.

Church is where I feel at home. Few things are more relaxing than preparing communion, which taught me how to pay attention to detail and to be thorough. Being on the Session made me a self starter with a great work ethic. I plan to continue to employ this work ethic and I intend to bring the same positive attitude, sincerity and effort in the future and in whatever capacity I serve my community, so that I make a good impact.

This essay is by a particularly devoted and sensitive young man. Often the idea of "home" sparks something in students. It's not just the house in which they live – home can be a feeling, an outside location, or even a person. The student didn't understand the purpose of the college essay at first and started with a format that sort of listed and described things he did or liked, but it wasn't purposeful and did not accurately reflect his passion or lived experience. Once we talked over who he is and what he cares about, the words just sort of flowed out of him and the essay appeared out of love for the topic.

The essay is actually a bit short, but it is complete. Short essays are better than long ones with extraneous words that do not add meaning or purpose to the work. One of the reasons it works is because it starts with a strong image that draws the reader into the story immediately. He is strong and specific about what he loves about church. He also reflects clearly and honestly on what he learned from his experiences at church and how he plans to put those lessons to use in the future. All of those elements in combination make for a successful essay. You won't be surprised to learn he is a journalism major and he got into his first-choice university with this essay.

Essay #2: A Passion Project

Reclaiming My Name

"There is an active shooter at a local synagogue in Squirrel Hill, Pittsburgh."

It was Saturday, October 27, 2018, Shabbat, the holiest day of the week. My city, my community, my religion, the synagogue where my parents got married; the synagogue where I attended a 50th wedding anniversary six weeks before; the synagogue that so many people called home, was under attack. I sat at home watching the news all day, feeling utterly stuck. There was nothing I could do to help my Jewish community in the moment, so I opened a Google Doc and wrote. I poured my heart out in a piece that eventually became my first publication on my school's newspaper. I wrote about gun violence, Antisemitism, the incompetence of our country's leadership, and my home in the Pittsburgh Jewish community.

On that fateful day in October, I was afraid. Afraid of being Jewish. My Jewish identity was under scrutiny. I didn't feel safe. I worried about the future of American Judaism. This tragedy that happened in my hometown reverberated throughout the entire world. The ripple effect is still happening today, including in my life. As I grappled with my identity, I discovered the power of words.

Three years later, I am now the photography editor and a writer for my high school's newspaper. I never knew I could write like how I did that day in 2018. I've always loved documenting the world around me, either on film, or through art, photography or music. But a new love came into the picture as well: writing. The paths I've taken throughout my life have led me to the field of journalism, but that moment of realization came from tragedy. That moment cemented my decision to explore this new path.

Also along this new path, I have strengthened my Jewish identity, and I was fortunate to travel to Israel on a life-changing journey last summer with 100 teens from around the US, Canada, and Israel.

On July 4, we visited the Western Wall. This two thousand year old wall represents resilience, determination, and chutzpah, the reason why Jews are still here. As I touched the wall for the first time, I broke down in tears. My thoughts and worries washed away.

One day in Jerusalem, I asked a shop owner on Ben Yehuda Street--a famous pedestrian mall--if he had a necklace with the name יוכבד (Yocheved) on it. My Hebrew name is Yocheved Hadassah. Yocheved was Moses's mother's name, and Hadassah comes from not only Queen Esther, a trailblazing Biblical Jewish woman, but from my great-grandmother Esther. Most Americans with unique Hebrew names would have to specially order their name on a necklace, but this shop owner had one with my Hebrew name on hand. It filled me with so much joy and pride. The accumulation of all the meaningful experiences on my trip and the idea that Jews have a place in the world where we can feel safe were solidified by this little moment: finding my name on a necklace.

There is so much power in a name. Names show your history, your ancestry, and your heritage. I am named after numerous strong women. I am proud of all of these things. Three years ago, my identity shattered. I feared for what being a Jew in America meant for my future and the future of our people. But today, I wear my necklace with pride every day. My Jewish identity is stronger than ever. It drives everything I do.

No one should ever fear their own identity. That is why I have dedicated my life to uplifting the voices of others. That's what journalism is--giving a voice to the voiceless. I write not only for myself, but for my community, via my perspective. Words have power. Names have power. Three years ago during that fateful October, my name was scrutinized. Today, I've reclaimed my name.

The student who wrote this essay is a young woman who not only feels deeply, but had her passions ignited out of an event that happened to her and around her. Not everyone has a particular event that rouses such passion, but she was strong enough to make a horrible event into something good for the world and her future. When she started writing, the essay had a lot of writing about her issues with anxiety and some other, more personal things. She also listed some accomplishments and was not using her space effectively. It was not until she gathered the courage to discuss her real passions, what fuels them, and who she really is deep down inside that the essay really took shape.

One of the reasons the essay works so well is that it comes to the tragic events via her own lens. She is not merely recounting events and their myriad of effects on her, but rather she focuses on what came out of the tragedy, how it fueled her toward a purpose, and what she hopes to do with that purpose. The essay is strong and specific.

In addition, this essay combines a few topics skillfully. There's the element of tragic events, but also her trip to Israel along with some family references and passion projects – all in one essay that flows beautifully. This proud young woman had a hard time choosing between colleges that admitted her.

Essay #3: What Will I Do Next?

The Brain

"OMG, that is so you," my friends exclaimed when I showed them the sticker I had recently bought. It was a picture of the brain—one half was black and white with computer code written in the background, while the other half was full of vibrant colors and random doodles.

Ever since I learned about the brain in AP Psychology, I have always been interested and fascinated by it. Instead of having a craving for chocolate or Chick-Fil-A, I have a craving to learn more about the brain, what it does, and how it affects us, which is why I bought a sticker for my computer that shows the difference between the left brain and the right brain and also why I have a coloring book of the anatomy of the brain. I long to study the brain, but why is it my main focus?

I think the answer to this question lies in the fact that I relate to the brain.

The brain is in charge of your whole body; it is like the nucleus of a cell or the CEO of a company. Ever since I can remember, I have always had the urge to speak up and take charge of a situation, but for most of my life I have never had the confidence to do so. Instead, I would step back and allow the person who always is the leader to take control over the situation. As I grew and discovered my strengths, my confidence grew exponentially, and so did my leadership skills. At my school, I am now known as a leader, someone a teacher can go to and know that they will get the task done, and someone who can motivate and organize a group around a common goal. The brain is an integral part of the body, while I am a vital component of my school and my community around me.

In order for the brain to be successful in controlling the body, it has to be able to balance the left hemisphere and the right hemisphere. The left side is in charge of more logical things, like solving a complex derivative or completing a Sudoku, while the right side deals with the creative side of things, such as taking a picture or daydreaming. Just as the brain has to, I have to balance two sides of my personality so that I can be the best version of myself— the most successful.

One of my "sides" consists of a hardworking person who is extremely organized and does not give up when faced with nearly impossible tasks, while the other part of me is someone who is the complete opposite of quiet – a person who is very outgoing, very random, and always has an opinion. All of these characteristics are what make me, me, but they have to be in perfect equilibrium in order to achieve my identity. If I was more studious than happy and sociable, I would not have any fun in the world, but if I was too outgoing and crazy, I would not have the many academic opportunities that I do today. I need both sides of my personality in the same way that the brain needs both the right and left hemispheres. Without them working together, you wouldn't be able to form a complete thought or have proper motor skills, and without both sides of my personality, I would not be who I am today.

The brain is still one of the most mysterious things on the planet, with functions that even our most talented scientists have not yet discovered. Just like the brain, I do not know everything about myself, but one thing that is for certain is that I will study the brain and hopefully in the process discover more of who I am.

Though many students do not exactly know what to choose for their major in college when they are still in high school, this particular student had a very clear idea of what she wanted to study. She has a clear goal, but this essay is so much more than the standard

"What I want to do with my life?" essay. She skillfully combines her fascination with studying the brain and correlates it with learning more about herself and her own likes and dislikes, goals, and ambitions.

One of the main reasons the essay works is that it has such a clear and unique voice. The writer pokes a little fun at herself, uses typical teen tropes, and lets the readers know that while she is serious about her work and interests, she doesn't take herself too seriously. She also allows room for growth because while she is focused on her point and her goals, she understands they are not fixed and that there is still room for her to change her mind if needed. So if you had to nail down a topic for the essay, it might be brain and brain research, but also it's about discovery and self-discovery in particular. This student attended a large research university where she had ample opportunities to connect with professors, work in labs, and fulfill her dreams.

Essay #4: A Value System

To Touch The Sky

The pink and orange sky was so beautiful that it looked as though it was a painting, the colors mixed and faded together a little too perfectly. I sat on the grass looking at the sky wanting nothing more than to be asleep, since I usually am at 4 am. Thirty-two girls sat all around me and together we sat in silence for a while and then talked. Thirty-two girls in one coherent conversation, no one talking over each other, no set or planned organization, just one flowing conversation. Over the past month we had gotten to know each other so deeply that despite the fact that our time together had come to an end, we felt no need to do anything extravagant. Usually people throw big goodbye parties when they have to leave their friends as a way to shove in more memories before it all ends, but at camp we did not feel a need to do that; the quiet time was enough.

Once the sun had fully risen, my friend and I walked back to our cabin to get some food. We were so tired from not sleeping all night that neither of us spoke for a long time. That was all that happened on my last night of camp; it was not crazy or thrilling, but the night was so much more memorable than it may seem. The genuine friendship my camp friends and I share is what makes simple nights full of silence significant. When someone has a genuine connection with one person or a group of people, it makes them feel like they are part of something bigger than themselves and that feeling alone is powerful enough to make silence equal to a million words.

When my parents came to pick me up, my month of technology hiatus that I enjoyed with my friends, that I have enjoyed for the past 9 summers, was over. My friends and I rushed towards each other, sobbing into each other's arms for the last few moments we had together, perplexed by the fact that we are sadder to leave camp than we were to leave home a month prior.

As I hugged my friends goodbye I knew that I would be able to keep in touch with them through social media, yet my heart still sank a bit with the thought of it. I was not going to see their real faces, personalities, or thoughts, I was going to see what they wanted them to be. On social media people tend to mimic personalities they see online, edit their photos, and make their life seem like something it is not, making it impossible to tell who they truly are behind their screen. At camp there is no way to hide or edit anything, allowing me to make friends naturally and through my true self. The main product of this is genuineness in friendships, conversations, and myself at camp is that it has become something I have strived and searched for in other areas of my life too.

Genuineness may not be something I constantly portray - I am a teenager after all - but it has become something that I highly value. I would always rather get to know someone through conversations and experiences with them, not by scrolling through their posted photos and messages. Something I have noticed about my generation is that we have become slaves to our phones, becoming further shackled with every social media post, app, and notification. I am in no way trying to bash my generation; I am very grateful to grow up in a time in which innovation, social justice, and opportunity is growing as well, but because of everything camp has taught me about friendship, my goal has become to break those shackles and to attempt to make genuine connections in all my future endeavors, classes, and careers.

The young woman who wrote this essay has an extraordinary sense of herself, an appreciation of the world around her, and the ability to be calm and practical in situations that would drive other teenagers to distraction. Her essay reflects a bit of that wisdom, and the way she can explain her value system is nothing short of amazing. True reflection involves not only telling what happened, but why it matters, what it means, and even what might be done differently next time. A good college essay, as I have noted before, covers all of that, but also includes something about the student that can only be explained via stories and explanations of who that person really is at his or her core.

What makes this essay work is the student's ability to describe events and show the reader the scene she is remembering. Then in the sense of true reflective practice, she is able to tell the reader precisely why it matters so much and how she has taken that event and held on to it to make meaning in her life and move forward. It shows precisely what matters to her as a person and why. This student chose to attend a wonderful school in a place that allows her to connect fully with the world around her.

Essay #5: History Makes the Man

Learning On Top Of The World

It was silent, save for the tired crunch of rubber and gravel, and the baited breaths that ricocheted against the barren summit. Fourteen hours since starting out, 3700 meters in the air, and neither my jaw nor my legs could stay up. The rising sun gleamed through the clouds, a bloodied pearl shooting off streams of color through the icy, empty air. It was four thirty in the morning, and the summit of Mount Fuji was warming up with the first light of day.

For a brief speck in time, everything else melted away. I could not feel the grainy dust that blanketed my feet, nor could I feel my lungs as they gasped for what little oxygen could be grasped from the air.

During my middle school years, which began in Bentonville, Arkansas, and ended in Chōfu, Tokyo, Japan, I didn't have great vision. Glasses helped my nearsightedness, but not with my vision for the future. When moving from Bentonville, a town of 20,000, in a state of 3 million people, to Tokyo, a city of 35 million, I only saw how hard it would be leaving my home country, and how hard it would be learning Japanese. What I couldn't see was what an incredible experience living in Japan could and would be.

I had the chance to climb Mount Fuji two weeks before starting high school. When I began the two-mile vertical journey, I didn't yet comprehend what an unbelievable opportunity I had. As I started to make my way up the sloping switchbacks, my mind was focused on how tired I thought I was. Through eight hours of hiking up and over

Fuji-san, I still didn't appreciate where I was. I was half way up the tallest mountain in Japan, and my mind was on the rough, rocky path, the thinning air, and how much easier it would be to be back home in bed.

Those eight hours put my mom, my dad, and me at the eighth station, 3250 meters up, and at our rest stop for a few hours. Perhaps it was the lack of oxygen in the air, but as my breath slowed, my mind began to feel clear for the first time. We had two hours to sleep before setting out again, but I couldn't sleep a wink. I was exhausted, but pulsating adrenalin would not let me drift off. We started hiking again just after midnight, four hours away from the summit. The path was lit by headlamps, bobbing up and down, a trail of fireflies, shrinking into just a few specks of light near the top. Each breath felt empty, but with each step I became less aware of how exhausted I was and more aware of exactly where I was. I neared the summit, and the first light began to peak over the clouds. I truly understood it for the first time: I was incredibly lucky. At the age of fourteen I had experienced more of the world than most people ever see.

Standing there at the top, my glasses were smeared with dirt and clouded with radiating steam that was coming off of me, but I could see farther than ever before. I could see miles of rock, clouds, and millions of trees. I can't say I had a magical epiphany, illuminating the secrets of the universe, but in that moment, I had to stop and think about just how few other teenagers would have the chance to summit Mount Fuji before starting high school. With that realization, I wasn't so tired anymore; the hike up didn't feel like as much of a challenge. I knew I had an opportunity few would have. With high school starting in just a couple of weeks, I had to start appreciating and taking advantage of everything I had. I wasn't going to let a single opportunity go to waste.

The student who wrote this essay had the extraordinary experience of living in various situations in his life, all before the age of 18. From small-town America to a sprawling Asian city, to a mid-size American city, he had it all covered. It was difficult for him to land on a topic that expressed his enthusiasm and his willingness to try new things, even when it was difficult. Then, once he landed on the topic, finding a way to combine the experience with the meaning he took from it was quite a trick.

The reason this essay works is that he meaningfully combines description with reflection. He trusts the reader in many places to understand what he is saying via the recounting of the climbing experience, but then in other spots, he fully explains what the experience meant to him. The hard part of writing is to know which spots require explanation and which do not.

While this particular student excelled in many areas in high school, he truly enjoyed math and science, yet that indication is not present in the essay at all. That's a very good thing, though, because the essay is meant to be about the student, his personality, and his values, and not what he likes to do or what he's good at. It is representative of him in general. Not only did this student graduate from a prestigious university, but he is also pursuing a Ph.D. in Astrophysics.

Essay #6: Personal History

Identity

A few years ago in Bulgaria, I was at a restaurant with my family. The waiter approached me and asked what I'd like to drink.

"I'll have a Coke," I said in perfect Bulgarian.

He shook his head.

"Okay... a Sprite then."

He shook his head again.

"Well what kind of soda do you have?" I asked.

"Coke and Sprite"

That's when it hit me. I had forgotten it was reversed in Bulgaria. Nodding means no and shaking your head means yes.

Though I have only been to Bulgaria a few times, it has always been a large part of my identity. Soon after my mom moved to the US, my grandparents followed suit. They live nearby so I'm constantly eating traditional Bulgarian foods that my grandma cooks. Banitsa, a filo pastry filled with feta cheese, is a favorite of mine. My grandparents sent me to a Bulgarian school, which I attended every Saturday afternoon from kindergarten up until senior year. There, I became immersed in Bulgarian history, literature and culture and made lifelong friends and connections. It wasn't all just work though. Every Bulgarian holiday we'd have a festive celebration filled with folk dances, traditional clothes and delicious food! They even had a piano at the school and since I played, I'd always perform various folk songs at the assemblies. This brings me to the next part of my identity: the piano.

I cannot remember my life before piano. That's how ingrained it was in me from early on. I remember listening to my mom play and dancing to the sound of the music. Both my parents are pianists so coming from this musical family - with 5 pianos in our house - I was naturally expected to play. And I became deeply passionate about it. Sure, the practicing is tough and the hours are long, but when you finally get up on the stage and hear the beautiful music you're making, it makes it all worth it. However, it wasn't the crowds or the prizes that made me fall in love with piano - it was the sense of family. Getting to hear my dad perform live or playing a duet with my mom - those were the things that mattered most to me. During the holidays, we sit at the piano and play Christmas songs before opening the presents. Some families will have game nights or movie nights, but for us, piano was that force that brought us together.

A couple years ago, I probably would've told you I wanted to be a pianist. Now? I don't feel quite the same way anymore. How come? After all, I love the piano and have been playing for almost all my life. And I guess that's just it. It's all I've ever known. As I continue my college education, I want to discover more about myself. To expand my horizons. Piano and Bulgaria are the two halves of my identity and are a constant reminder of everything I love about home. I'll always be looking forward to eating my grandma's banista or playing Christmas songs with my parents. However, no one is defined by just two things. Now I have a chance to really learn what makes me tick. Whether it be trying new clubs, studying new fields, or finding something about myself I wouldn't have before. That's what makes these college years so special. And no matter what path I take or what lies ahead - piano and my Bulgarian heritage will consistently be a part of my life. Of my identity.

This young man has a very specific story to tell about his background and identity that is not immediately clear from the other parts of his application – the activities resume or the transcript. This crucial piece of who he is can only appear in the essay. The problem, he found, is that there are two stories he needs to tell about his background to give Admissions people a full picture of himself and so, integrating them was a bit of an issue. Then he had to work on an exciting opener that worked for the entire essay as well.

The reason this essay works is that it takes various stories and puts them together into a cohesive whole. He wrote many versions of the stories and then after they were satisfactory, he wrote the connective tissue to tie it all together. This method is not for everyone, and there are definite pitfalls that can happen, but when it works, it's really wonderful. This student is doing beautifully at his top choice school.

Essay #7: Passion

The Sea And The Board

I scan the horizon, perched atop my board, bobbing in the cold Pacific water. "Just one more good one, then I'm done," I tell myself. The truth is, I've said that for the last five waves, but with each wave better than the last, I couldn't allow myself to leave. That's just how my brain works - no matter what I'm doing, I feel the constant need to improve, to do just one more, and to ignore the voice in my head telling me to stop. A swell appears in the distance, a small ripple in the vast ocean, but I have learned to recognize this pattern. Through hours and hours of practice, my brain is able to understand that this small swell will turn into a surfable wave by the time it reaches me, and my mind shifts to one focus -- catching the wave.

The wave grows as it approaches, rolling forward with natural grace. My tired body flops down onto the board, water spraying onto my stony face. Water flows across the board as I am propelled through the water by the paddling motion I've done so many times. The wave is still distant, but I've made my way to the optimal takeoff point -- ensuring the best possible ride. I find that this little bit of extra work, even if it only yields an extra two seconds on the ride, is worth it. I motivate myself to work harder and do more; the payoff will be worth it in the long term.

My hands move through the water at a furious pace, launching my board through the water to match the speed of the wave. Swiveling my head to look behind me reveals a towering wave about to break on top of me. My dad's words ring through my head, "Panicking has never helped anyone. Never panic." This sentiment has helped me get through countless tough situations and has played a major role in the person I have become. I try to be methodical with every decision I make, to take the time to understand all of my options and formulate an informed opinion on how to respond. As I lay on my board, a few feet in front of the inevitably crashing wave, I stay calm.

A monumental surge of energy flows beneath me, a living testament to the sheer power of the earth. I pop to my feet, standing atop six feet of coordinated fast flowing water -- a wave. My legs shake, losing their balance on the board as I begin a steep drop down the face of the wave. My arms flail, desperately reaching for the balance I had known just one second before. Whether by sheer luck or some sort of unknown genius, I regain my balance, the wind breaking across my face as I fly down the face of the wave.

My head clears, my body relaxes, and euphoria washes over me as I turn my board parallel to the wave. A section of the wave opens up ahead of me, and an idea for a trick formulates in my head. I think to myself, "I see the pros do this all the time, how hard could it be?" My confidence soars as my board angles up the wave and whips back around. No matter what I'm doing, I will always look to challenge myself. In order for me to make real progress, I have found that I must take risks, test my boundaries, and not be afraid of failure.

In an instant, I am launched off of my board, flying through the air until my back slams against the water, sending a wave of pain up my body. The wave throws my limp body over the falls, and I crash back down to the water unable to move, my limbs being tossed around by the relentless power of the wave. Thirty seconds feels like a lifetime in these conditions, and my empty lungs long for air. Eventually, the wave rolls past me, and I am met with a feeling of relief as my head pops out of the water. I drag my exhausted body back on top of my board. My sore shoulders beg me to stop paddling, but I fight the pain and let my hands take me back out to sea. I regain my perch on the board. "Last one," I tell myself. "For real this time."

This essay, by a very interesting young man, does something that perhaps not all essays can pull off: it discusses one single event. To the author, the event was not only pivotal but representative. He shows the reader his strength, perseverance, attention to detail, and even in a small way, his excellent relationship with his father. The student skillfully lets the reader know that this one description is about more than just catching a wave; it's about who he is as a person underneath the action of surfing.

The reason this essay in particular works is that it is transparent. A reader does have to work to gather the meaning, but the reward of knowing who the student is through his actions makes the reader feel close to the writer as he or she understands the depth of what has been written. Writing a college essay this way is not for everyone, but when it does work, it can be beautiful. The student attends a prestigious university in Europe.

Essay #8: Family Ups and Downs

Dad

"Dad we've been this way before. We're going in a circle"
"Alana Grace I know where I'm going"

Uh oh, my middle name - a sure sign I annoyed him. I came to find out that roaming around in Venice isn't the time for family bonding. My dad and I passed the same street sign at least five times in a row before realizing we were hopelessly lost. I begged my dad to ask locals for directions. He never wants to admit that he's a tourist and tries to assimilate into any culture. I never understood this. It's like the khaki shorts and bass fishing cap didn't give it away. After all the arguing, his steps paced quicker than mine. The silence was tense. It seemed as if my help was only angering him more.

I realized that this bickering, although new to me, would be happening more often in the future than what I was familiar with. I didn't spend much time with my father in the past. My parents divorced when I was five years old and I had grown up seeing him only every other weekend.

I spent my time with my mom and grandma. Every day I fogged up the window waiting for my mother to come home and give me a big, wet kiss of jungle red across my forehead. On summer days, we laid out in the sun as she told me stories of living in France, dreaming of taking me. The plane ticket never made it into her hands but she hoped I would be able to experience what she did. During the school year, I came home to my grandmother's embrace hugs, squeezing me till I had no air. Her bubbly smile always made me feel so safe and loved.

Locked away in my room at the apartment, the frustration with my dad made me wonder what was missing for us to feel like a father and daughter. My life and family were changing. My mother had one month left to live after fighting two rounds of cancer, and my grandmother passed away the year before. The family I beloved slipped through my fingers; my safety and comfort felt shattered.

Months after my mother passed, I still felt unmoored from the heartbreak but I decided to reach out to the family I still had left, my dad. As I asked more questions and found out more about him, our shared love of traveling brought us a connection that we held on to. Still missing my mom, I made the best of my situation. He was trying too.

Two years later, my father and I visited the Atacama Desert in Chile. The landscape looked as if it were a scene from Mars. Within minutes of wandering down hills of reddish sand, strong winds started stirring. Sand blocked our view, striking our face, arms, and legs. My dad took out a beach towel in his backpack and used it to cover us. We raced back to the van, having handfuls of sand in every crease of our clothing. We slammed the sliding door, blocking sand flying in. Out of breath, we sat in shock of what just happened. I sighed. I sat to get a hold of my breath. My dad turned to me, let out a long sigh, then a burst of laughter. I laughed with him, gasping for air as we laughed driving back to our hotel. That day felt like I met the man I've known my whole life.

Our relationship will never be perfect but the wall between my father and me comes down brick by brick. In the past, I knew him as my weekend dad. Now I know him as an important friend in my life. I've grown to look beyond the reality of my grief and for the silver lining of the new bond I've established with my father.

Not every student has a story so gripping to tell like this one does, but she uses her story very creatively. She does not want to talk about the losses in her life that have affected every part of her but instead chooses to focus on the healing, the silver lining, and the ways her mother is still with her through it all. She does a wonderful job of staying on point with the essay regarding not only what is happening at the jumping-off point but also reflecting on its strong meaning.

This essay works because it embodies the overcoming part of a challenge. When a student writes about a challenge, the Admissions Committee has an eye on how they overcome it and less on the actual event. Resilience is important to show – as well as hard work. Rather than feeling bad for the student, the Admissions Committee can come away from this essay admiring her and her drive to push forward. This student is at a highly regarded public university and thriving.

Essay #9: Family and Learning

To Jump In The Lake

It's a brutally hot day—80 degrees of sweltering heat. I'm at my grandparents' house in the middle of nowhere, Pennsylvania. I'm sitting in the bed of my aunt's truck, waiting impatiently for my cousins to hop in. Finally, my two cousins, Madigan and Jack, and my sister, Julia, jump in. "Took you long enough," I grumble. "My hair turned grey waiting for you." My sister shakes her head, used to my antics, but my cousins laugh. "It's good to see someone still appreciates humor," I mutter to myself.

The truck rumbles into life and we take the shaky trip down the gravel driveway, laughing at every bump. As we pull out on to the main road to Black Moshannon State Park, the truck picks up speed. The wind, blessedly cold, picks my hair up and carries away any chance of conversation. We rocket down the road that shadows the lake, past the picnic tables, the ranger station, and the dock. Time to do something fun. My first bridge jump—a momentous event in any young man's life.

As we get closer to the bridge, my excitement builds, and my worries melt away. My aunt's voice suddenly pulls me out of my daydream. "Get down," she hollers through the open window, as the ranger station rapidly approaches. I duck down. Technically, it's illegal to ride in the truck bed. Who would've thought.

We pull into the parking lot at the beach. I hop down from the truck bed and hike up my swimsuit. We trudge over to the sidewalk that crosses the bridge, nervous grins on our faces. I'll be honest, I'm quite nervous. What if the ranger comes along? What if the water is too shallow? What if someone reports us? But of course, I cover those nerves in a hard façade of manly bravado. When there's a gap in the cars crossing the bridge, my aunt, in her strongest stage whisper, calls "Now." Game time. We sprint up to the side of the bridge, my sister, cousins, and I united in this mad dash. We cross the barrier and spread along the railing.

I look down. That was a mistake—heights and I don't have the best relationship. Gulp. If we don't jump now, someone will see us, I think to myself. I look left. My cousin Madigan, who always laughs at my jokes and summons ghosts with the Ouija board, looks back. I look right. My cousin Jack, the brother I never had, who always roughhouses with me and makes inappropriate jokes about my grandfather's lack of hair, looks back. I look down. The murky unknowns of the cold water below stare back. I steel my nerves. I jump.

I splash into the freezing water, the warmth running out of my body. Success. "Get to the truck," my aunt shouts from the shore. Gladly obeying, I swim to the shore. I hop in the truck, shivering, and settle in for the ride back.

No cell service, no hospitals, and most definitely no Dunkin Donuts down the street. Why? Why do I keep coming back?

To learn. At Black Moshannon, I am surrounded and supported by those I love and those who love me. It is an escape from the rigidity of school, life, and social expectations, and an opportunity for some healthy rebellion. Here, I learn life skills never taught in school. I learned how to start a fire and make tea, I found my first set of antlers, I found my first bear prints, I got over my fear of heights, I set off my first fireworks, I won my first boat race, and I learned to drive. Most importantly, I learned that opportunities to learn new things are all around me. All it takes is the courage to ask a question—the courage to steel my nerves and commit to something new.

This student has a very strong family tradition that defines him. He uses that tradition and the attached meaning to craft an essay that is both descriptive and reflective. The student had incredible success in high school with grades, sports, activities, and even religious events, but none of those things could really explain to an Admissions Committee that he is funny, curious, and at times, sarcastic. He needed a place to show them that he is more than what he does and can accomplish and that he can form relationships, find meaning in his family, and connect to the greater world in a significant way. It's almost like he uses the essay as a way to "humanize" himself.

The student is finding further success at an Ivy League school where he continues to make meaning through connections, activities, and his high spirits.

Essay #10: Cultural Awareness

The Meaning Of Independence

Move-in day had arrived. Standing in the midst of the chaos, I watched my mother and sister lug boxes into my sister's dorm room. The bed needed assembly; the clothes needed hanging; and the food needed organizing. While trying to complete one task, I got distracted by the next incoming task. Unlike my sister and me, my mother was simultaneously unloading, organizing, and cleaning without breaking a sweat. After moving to the U.S. from Syria, she has had plenty of practice with moving in and out of homes. A knock at the door announced a crowd of welcoming students. I glanced at my mother and the woman who, moments before, was our rock holding down the fort, was now in a state of panic. As a traditional Syrian woman who was placed into an arranged marriage at the age of 18, she has a limited viewpoint of different cultures. While my sister and I saw a group of welcoming students, my mom saw an invasion of privacy. She glared at my sister and called in Arabic, "Why are these people in your room? This is where you are going to sleep!". Moments after, her eyes met their shoes which they had all failed to remove before coming in. Before she could lose her composure, my sister and I swiftly removed the crowd from the room. Through my mother's eyes, these students, who only had good intentions, had completely disrespected her.

My awareness of my bicultural upbringing became apparent when I started going to school. After getting awkward stares from my classmates, I realized that speaking Arabic and eating traditional Syrian food weren't the norm. And during Ramadan, the fasting students were required to sit amongst the others who were eating in the cafeteria. The minimal Muslim representation at my school meant that it took me multiple attempts to allow a room where fasting students could sit during lunch. After hearing about my difficulties, my mom's face filled with disappointment when she realized that I have a drastically different childhood than she had. Her upbringing mirrors the life of my extended family in Syria. There, the women of the family value a successful marriage over an education or a career. They focus on being efficient in the house and skilled at cooking and cleaning. The mere fact that I drive a car shocks them.

While a teenager having a job and a driver's license is ordinary in the U.S., my mother always thought it was strange that I was so independent at a young age. However, my independence is a direct product of growing up with her. Even her language barrier taught me life skills that I wouldn't otherwise have. By the time I was ten years old, I was setting up my own doctor's appointments and calling the television company when there were issues. My definition of independence transformed from being someone that I could rely on, to being someone that my mother could rely on.

Being a first-generation Syrian American woman means that I see the world through multiple lenses. When the students barged into my sister's dorm, I recognized their kind intentions while also understanding my mother's reaction. And at school, I can clearly spot the lack of support towards minority cultures. While I sometimes wish that I could experience the full immersion that my mother had, living in the U.S. allows me to share my Syrian culture with those around me. I'm also able to share my experiences in America with my family in Syria. Growing up alongside my mom while she was adapting to a new life allowed me to learn her life lessons with her. She taught me to be resilient even when she wasn't familiar with the language or customs of those around her. Moving forward, I will carry my bicultural lifestyle with pride to remember how it strengthened and shaped me.

Sometimes, a student's background is important and has to be addressed in the essay because it is so illuminating for the Admissions Committee. A student can have a background that is very interesting and diverse, and the Admissions Committee would never know it if it is not addressed in the essay. In the case of this student, being a Saudi Arabian woman shaped the way she sees and experiences the world. Her mother, a role model of strength for the student, is also sometimes bewildered by the way American society works. The student would be remiss in not telling the Admissions Committee how her family life and background has shaped her.

This essay works because it opens with a strong story that illustrates a cultural difference but specifically takes place in an American context like moving the student's older sister into a dorm. The student is able to make the cultural difference apparent to everyone but still explain why it is all significant to her and her family's circumstances. Her sister's move-in story is typical in some ways, but atypical in others. The student skillfully describes the experience in terms readers can relate to, but then reflects and shows readers how it is actually different.

This student is attending the school of her dreams and doing well – culturally and academically.

Essay #11: Independence

Grit And Determination - A Proud Daughter

My parents were definitely unconvinced that leaving for a quarter of my Junior year was a great idea, so I sent them a short and clear message: "Rafi from the school in Israel is coming Sunday, so please be ready." If anyone could convince my parents to let me go to Israeli boarding school, it was Rafi.

My parents attended the meeting, learned the unique opportunities of the trip, and the ability to continue my school work. However, they were still on edge as it was very expensive. I spent the next few weeks applying for scholarships, which I then received.

Six months later I was off to Israel, traveling to a foreign country alone. Over eight weeks the country became my classroom. However, I also had to do my own laundry, manage time and money, and handle my regular classes on top of my Israel studies classes, all without outside direction. The Israel trip and all of the planning it took to get there, enhanced my independence and determination, which started a few years prior with the Leukemia and Lymphoma Society (LLS).

When I was eleven, my mom had Non-Hodgkin's Lymphoma. Our family lived in Japan at the time, and my mom took treatment in the U.S, so I lived eight months without a mother. My mom always had groceries delivered, but without her, I started going to the grocery store on Sundays with my dad. I stopped taking violin lessons because my dad couldn't come home early enough to take my brother and me. I walked to school by myself for the first time.

While my mom was sick, I learned about LLS, an organisation that raises money for blood cancer research. A year later my mom was cancer-free, coinciding with the year of my bat-mitzvah. I wanted to incorporate the LLS in my bat-mitzvah service project, so I decided to organise a "Light the Night" walk in Tokyo, a fundraising walk that takes place in the U.S. but not in Japan.

I wrote hundreds of emails asking people to participate. The LLS sent over their signature lanterns from the U.S. and that night I raised $9000 for cancer research. I walked next to my mother, proud daughter of a survivor.

I reached out to the LLS my freshman year, having moved back to the U.S. after spending most of my life in Japan. My best friend and I formed a team to enter the Students of the Year Campaign, where teams of High School students raise as much money as possible over seven weeks. I contacted multiple companies and spoke to CEOs, managers and presidents, letting them know about the goals and mission of the LLS, and why it was personal to me. My Uncle Neil was president of his own company, and before he would donate, he put me through my paces. I prepared talking points and made a presentation on my goals for the campaign; he wouldn't give me a break because I was his niece. He made a sizable donation and I learned the art of presenting a good case.

By the end of the campaign we raised over $50,000, giving my team the opportunity to name a research grant in honor of my mother. This award reflects my mother's strength in defeating cancer, the hours of work I put into raising money, and lastly, turning the hardships of cancer into something positive. Now, through my efforts, there is research being done in her name.

My mom's cancer shaped my life. Running my own successful fundraising campaign at fifteen gave me confidence, so when the opportunity arose to go to Israel, I was ready. At eleven, I took responsibilities and moved towards independence. I wouldn't wish cancer on any family, but I am thankful for my mom's recovered health and for the lessons I learned because of it.

This student had A LOT to say because a lot of things happened to her in her short life, so the trick was handling it all thematically in one essay. The theme is independence, so over the course of all of the events she describes, she goes back to the one, overarching idea that everything that happened and everything she did, led her to be a more independent person, capable of handling things.

This essay works because the theme allows it to "hang together" well and not sound disjointed. She can get everything she wants into the essay and have readers understand how the experiences shaped her in one specific way – generating independence.

This student is happily attending her first-choice school.

Conclusion

I hope throughout this book, you have found ways to connect with the process of writing the college essay. Please do keep in mind that it is a process and something that you might enjoy and embrace if you can get into the right mindset. To finish, I would like to leave you with a few reminders:

- Your job is to get your unique personality onto the page for the main essay – show the readers, and the Admissions Officers, why they should choose you to attend their school over any other applicant.

- Prompts for the main essay exist mostly for convenience and are not something you have to abide by strictly. Write what feels good for you whether it answers a specific question or not.

- The exact opposite advice exists for the supplemental questions: always answer the exact question asked. Many of those questions come in parts so you have to address each part fully. There is a difference between the question "Why do you want to go to this school?" and "What excites you about being a student at this school?" The difference is subtle, but it exists – the first one asks a more general question and you can answer with a myriad of methods, but the second one must include information about academic programs to address the idea of being a student.

- You can re-use your answers to supplemental questions if you are strategic and careful. Always change the name of the school and/or program and professor to the correct one for that particular essay! Sometimes questions are nuanced and though two might seem the same, they need a few tweaks to fully answer the question asked by each school. A long supplemental essay for one school might be the basis for an Honors College essay at another school if revised well.

- COVID-19 was difficult for everyone but you need not answer the COVID-19 prompt if something unique did not happen to you.

This book is meant to get you started on your journey with writing your college essays and to get you thinking of the future beyond high school. I wish you great success with the process and that you can have a wonderful experience as you go through it. You are definitely set up for success! YOU CAN DO IT! Good luck!

www.ingramcontent.com/pod-product-compliance
Lightning Source LLC
Chambersburg PA
CBHW081740270326
41932CB00020B/3348